AN ALIEN PLACE

The Fort Missoula, Montana, Detention Camp
1941–1944

AN ALIEN PLACE

The Fort Missoula, Montana, Detention Camp

1941–1944

by Carol Bulger Van Valkenburg

LIBRARY OF CONGRESS CATALOG CARD NO. 95-069646

ISBN 0-929521-99-4

First Printing July 1995

Book Design & Typography: Arrow Graphics
Cover Design: Bill Vaughn

PICTORIAL HISTORIES PUBLISHING COMPANY, INC.
713 South Third Street West, Missoula, MT 59801

For Fred, Kevin and Kristin

ACKNOWLEDGMENTS

IN ADDITION TO members of my family, I am grateful for the help and support of many people. The late Warren Brier, former dean of the University of Montana School of Journalism, was especially helpful in preparation of the original manuscript. Those who gave their assistance in the editing were Jim Lopach, Tom Bulger and Mary Lou Tobin. To many of my friends and colleagues I owe thanks for their advice, assistance or just their good humor: Anne Murphy, Jerry Holloron, Charlie Hood, Bob McGiffert, Dennis Swibold, Patty Reksten and Joe Durso. And to my fishing pals, Dennis, John Bulger, Greg Tollefson and Larry LaCounte, who help me remember what life is all about.

CONTENTS

INTRODUCTION

How did the quiet college town of Missoula, Montana, nestled in the shadow of a mountain range at the confluence of the Clark Fork, Blackfoot and Bitterroot rivers, come to house more than a thousand Italian aliens and another thousand Japanese whose loyalties were suspect?

The story begins in another century, during an era when this nation's government was at war with an earlier enemy, the American Indian. As white settlers took over tribes' traditional homelands and hunting grounds, conflicts with the Indians grew fierce. The government tried to push Indian tribes onto ever-smaller reservations but many bands resisted. One anonymous military historian set the scene like this:

"The main tribe of the Nez Perces, principally located in Idaho, had long been on friendly terms with the whites. Chief Joseph, called the Napoleon of the Reds, and Chief Looking Glass held the restless band in check. However, the settlers abused the reds, stealing their stock, and cheating them in trades whenever possible. After the unjust imprisonment of one of the tribal officials by the soldiers, the young impetuous braves could no longer be restrained . . . ."[1]

Fearing skirmishes with the Nez Perce, Flatheads, Pend Oreille and Kootenai, Montana's congressional delegation pushed for the establishment of a fort near Missoula, a small town situated at the mouth of Hellgate Canyon, from which the Clark Fork flowed. Col. Wesley Merritt was sent to select a site, and from the three he chose, the location southwest of town was selected. The first troops arrived in June of 1877, just two months before an infamous battle was to take place in the Big Hole Valley, southeast of Missoula.

When Chief Joseph, whose name was In-mut-too-yah-lat-lat (Thunder Traveling Over the Mountains), refused to be moved onto a reservation, soldiers attacked his band in Idaho. Joseph led his people into Montana, planning to escape to Canada. In the Bitterroot Valley, he made an agreement with two companies of soldiers sent from Fort Missoula, understanding that his people would be allowed to pass peacefully. But four days later, in the Big Hole Valley, troops from Fort Shaw, Montana, surrounded the Indians' camp and attacked at daybreak, killing 50 women and children and 30 fighting men. Joseph escaped with the remainder of his band, but was captured in the Bear Paw Mountains, not far from the Canadian border. It was here that he made his famous speech, "From where the sun now stands, I will fight no more forever."

Soon after the Big Hole battle, battalions of the Third Infantry from Alabama and Mississippi were ordered to Missoula. An arduous journey followed and the soldiers arrived to find that other than two log trading posts, the only structures at the site were cabins and two partially completed barracks. The troops went to work building a permanent encampment. Stone for the foundations was hauled from the foothills, while lumber came from a small mill in Pattee Canyon.

The soldiers at Fort Missoula were to engage in only one clash with Indians. In July 1878 a detachment led by Lt. Thomas Wallace pursued a band of Nez Perce that was trying to return from Canada. Several Indians were killed.

One battalion assigned to the fort in its early days consisted of Black soldiers from the Twenty-Fifth Infantry. It gained notoriety, not for fighting Indians, but for riding bicycles. Lt. James A. Moss organized a group of 23 of the soldiers for a 2,000-mile journey to St. Louis. Moss believed bicycles were a more efficient mode of travel for the cavalry than were horses and wagons, and meant to use the well-publicized trip to prove his point. Travel late in the 19th century was difficult under almost any circumstance, but this trip was both tortuous and torturous. Summer rains made the route nearly impassable and the men were often forced to lug their bicycles on their backs.

"For days there was alternate hot choking weather, and then flashing storms that stampeded the cattle in the hills. Men sprained their ankles and had to follow on foot. Rumors of rattlesnakes broke up comfortable camps and started the procession out in the middle of the night. Hail in drifts eight feet high blocked the road. Mud covered the wheels until they were discs of gumbo," according to one account of the trip.[2] The bicycle corps completed the trip but was soon reassigned when the Spanish-American war broke out.

There was no significant military use for the fort almost from its inception. Few troops were stationed at Fort Missoula over the years, though plenty of building took place. Much of the soldiers' work consisted of settling labor disputes involving miners, helping fight masssive forest fires and providing escorts for trains. But for the most part, it was a fort without a purpose.

During World War I the post became a training camp for mechanics, under the direction of the military and Montana State University in Missoula. Townspeople sought to have the fort turned over to the university, but the War Department declined. The Forest Service wanted it as a training site for pilots, but the War Department rejected that proposal, too.

In the 1930s the government agreed to use it for a district office for the Civilian Conservation Corps, and during that period more construction was undertaken. The camp was large enough so that in 1941 its many barracks and remote location made it an ideal site for a camp that would initially house Italian seamen, and later men whom the United States considered its most insidious enemies.

In the early months of 1941, President Franklin Roosevelt ordered the impoundment of Axis ships stranded in U.S. ports, and the government assumed custody of the crews. This act by the president would open a new chapter in the history of Fort Missoula. The men from these ships would soon find themselves at this old army post, where most would remain for the next three to four years.

The Italians sent to the fort had languished on merchant ships docked in U.S. ports from the time war broke out in Europe in late 1939. In 1941 the American government ordered the ships impounded when officials suspected that crewmen, on the orders of Axis governments, were sabotaging the ships. These nations apparently feared that the United States was about to take control of the vessels and turn them over to Great Britain to be used against the Axis in the war. When the United States seized the ships, it charged the crewmen with overstaying the limits allowed by their visas, an offense punishable by deportation. However, because the war prevented their safe return home, and because their ships were damaged and could not sail in any case, the men were sent to Fort Missoula.

Six months later, the Italians and a few Germans at the fort would be joined by a thousand Japanese. While most Americans are familiar with the details of the later mass movement of nearly 120,000 Japanese from the West Coast of the United States, the arrest and detention of hundreds of other Japanese in the weeks immediately following the bombing of Pearl Harbor has gone almost unnoticed and undocumented. These Japanese arrested in December 1941 and January and February 1942 were not men whom the United States government had proven were saboteurs or enemy agents. They were, for the most part, leaders of the Japanese community in America, people the government thought would be most influential should Japanese on the mainland organize against the United States.

Though many of these men were the most important and powerful Japanese who would be detained over the course of the war, little has been written about their arrests, hearings and detention. And because the United States government kept secret for 45 years the information about allegations of mistreatment of some of these men, little light has been shed on that shameful episode.

This book tells a bit about these men: who they were, how their lives took this peculiar turn, and how the tranquil town of Missoula, Montana, became for some, a shelter, and for others, a painful interlude in lives turned inside out by the events of a world war.

"CHE BELLA VISTA":
THE ITALIANS ARRIVE IN MISSOULA

G ERMANY'S CONQUEST of Poland in September 1939 began a war that would endure for six years and claim the lives of 45 million people. While the United States would not be thrust into World War II until December 7, 1941, Montana was to be nudged indirectly into the conflict six months before the attack at Pearl Harbor.

As war engulfed nation after nation in Europe, navigation of the oceans became increasingly hazardous. Hitler's invasion of Poland and Britain's subsequent declaration of war against Germany and its ally, Italy, left many German and Italian seamen unwittingly stranded in United States ports in the waning months of 1939. The British government refused to grant safe passage through international waters for any ships carrying able-bodied men from nations with which Britain was at war.[1] For more than a year the ships' crews sat idle. In the winter of 1941 reports began to appear in the press that crews of some of the ships from Axis nations were sabotaging their own ships. Fires were set aboard some vessels and foreign objects were jammed into the gears of others. The Roosevelt administration said the crews were acting on the orders of their governments.[2]

On the last weekend in March, President Roosevelt, using the authority of the 1917 espionage act that made it a crime to damage a ship, whether foreign or domestic, harbored in the territorial waters of the United States, ordered 69 German, Italian and Danish vessels seized. The 775 Italian seamen and 100 German sailors aboard the ships were taken into "protective custody." Danes aboard 35 Danish ships were allowed to remain on board.

U.S. Attorney General Robert H. Jackson, who would later that year become a Supreme Court justice, explained why it was necessary for the United States to seize the ships, though this country was not at war:

"Under modern methods of warfare, the most critical period for a nation under attack is the period preceding the actual employment of military force. The secret weapon of the Nazis has been the failure of nation after nation to recognize and deal with this non-military invasion. Our statute law has in many respects failed to take into account this non-military period of attack."[3]

But Jackson's explanation was somewhat lame because the espionage act under which the government detained those ships permitted such detention only in times of emergency. The attorney general tried to make the case that while the law might not technically recognize this as an emergency, the history of Nazi aggression made it reasonably clear that the United States would be dragged into the war and that the pre-war period demanded a readiness that could constitute an emergency.

Facing page
An aerial view of Fort Missoula in the late 1930s before the internment camp was established. Part of the Missoula Country Club can be seen at the lower right.
PICTORIAL HISTORIES COLLECTION

Vol. 10, No. 15

LIFE

April 14, 1941

HERE YOU SEE THE FIRST USE OF U. S. ARMED FORCE IN WORLD WAR II.   IN BOSTON HARBOR, MARCH 30, COAST GUARDSMEN SEIZE GERMAN TANKER "PAULINE FRIEDERIC

U. S. USES FIRST FORCE TO WIN BLOODLESS VICTORY IN BATTLE OF THE ATLANTIC

In the winter of 1916-17 Teddy Roosevelt, Albert Bushnell Hart and other interventionists of that bygone day strenuously urged the U. S. Government to seize and make use of the 109 German merchant ships then lying at refuge in U. S. harbors. The ships were much needed, but President Wilson held back. Careful of the forms of neutrality, he feared the seizure might rouse the Kaiser to declare war. Not until the U. S. itself had formally declared war on Germany did U. S. armed forces, on April 6, 1917, pounce on the German ships.

The difference between President Roosevelt and President Wilson, and between U. S. "neutrality" of 1941 and that of 1917, was dramatically illustrated on March 30. Out from Washington went an order, approved by the President from the cruising *Potomac*. In 24 U. S. harbors from Portland, Me., to Grays Harbor, Wash. and south to the Canal Zone, Coast Guardsmen and soldiers armed with rifles and ma-

chine guns swiftly boarded 28 Italian, two German and 35 Danish merchant ships, carted their crews off to immigration stations or jails. In the Battle of the Atlantic, the U. S. had won a bloodless victory. The only show of resistance, a mild one, was by Italian crewmen at Jacksonville, Fla.

It was a historic act: the first use of U. S. armed force in World War II. Six months ago it would have been a screaming sensation throughout the land. Last week, significantly, the public reaction was one of general satisfaction, mingled with mild vexation that the thing had not been done sooner. Legal excuse for doing it now was a tip-off that the Italian and German crews had begun to sabotage their ships. The Espionage Act of 1917 authorizes seizure to prevent such action. Official explanation of the seizures of Danish ships, whose crews welcomed the invaders and were shortly allowed to go back aboard their undamaged ships, was that their ships

might shortly have been sabotaged by "other crews"

Legal or not, the U. S. move was tough stuff an recognized as such by the Axis press which screame "piracy" and "Wild West." That U. S. officials ha fully made up their minds to get tough and stay th way was shown by Secretary Hull's stiff rejection German and Italian diplomats' protests, by prepar tions to prosecute guilty Italian and German crev men for sabotage, by a stiff Hull note ordering th Italian naval attaché in Washington, Admiral A berto Lais, out of the country for having ordered hi countrymen's acts of sabotage. Whether the seize ships would be turned over directly to Britain, o used by the U. S. in place of American ships to turned over to Britain, remained officially unan nounced. But Secretary Hull did not leave man citizens guessing when, in answer to questions abou the ships' disposal, he reminded reporters that th U. S. policy is still all aid to Britain short of wa

The April 14, 1941, issue of *Life* magazine details the seizing of Italian, Danish and German ships in U.S. ports.

Life magazine stated the case in clearer terms: "In the winter of 1916–17 Teddy Roosevelt, Albert Bushnell Hart and other interventionists of that bygone day strenuously urged the U.S. Government to seize and make use of 109 German merchant ships then lying in refuge in U.S. harbors. The ships were much needed, but President Wilson held back. Careful of the forms of neutrality, he feared the seizure might rouse the Kaiser to declare war. Not until the U.S. itself had formally declared war on Germany did U.S. armed forces, on April 6, 1917, pounce on the German ships.

"The difference between President Roosevelt and President Wilson and between U.S 'neutrality' of 1941 and that of 1917, was dramatically illustrated on March 30. Out from Washington went an order, approved by the President from the cruising Potomac. In 21 U.S. harbors from Portland, Me., to Grays Harbor, Wash. and south to the Canal Zone, Coast Guardsmen and soldiers armed with rifles and machine guns swiftly boarded 28 Italian, two German and 35 Danish merchant ships, carted their crews off to immigration stations or jails. In the Battle of the Atlantic, the U.S. had won a bloodless victory."[4]

The magazine called it "a historic act" that six months earlier "would have been a screaming sensation throughout the land." But the reaction instead "was one of general satisfaction, mingled with mild vexation that the thing had not been done sooner." *Life* brushed off any legal questions with the comment that "legal or not" it was "tough stuff" and U.S. officials had "fully made up their minds to get tough and stay that way. . . ." The United States also ordered the Italian naval attache in Washington, Admiral Alberto Lais, out of the country for having ordered the acts of sabotage. What would be done with the ships? *Life* said Secretary of State Cordell Hull, asked about the ships' disposal, "did not leave many citizens guessing" when he "reminded reporters that the U.S. policy is still all aid to Britain short of war."[5]

There was little argument in Congress over the legality, where members acted swiftly to authorize seizure of the impounded ships. The House passed a bill on May 6, 1941, that would allow the United States to use "idle" foreign ships docked in U.S. ports for the nation's national defense.

As for the ships' crews, the United States issued formal warrants on April 1 charging the sailors with overstaying the sixty-day limit permitted of alien seamen in United States territories. The men were held pending deportation. Most were sent to Ellis Island to await a determination as to their fate.

By April 12 the U.S. Justice Department held 1,300 Italians in custody. Of that number, 483 were men from the luxury Italian liner *Conte Biancamano*, which had been stranded in the Panama Canal Zone for 18 months. One hundred and eighty-nine seamen had been indicted for sabotage of the *Biancamano* and were awaiting trial.[6]

Unable to return the other Italian seamen home, the Justice Department announced they would be housed at a former Army post outside Missoula, Montana.

Fort Missoula, established in 1877 to garrison cavalry troops whose duty it was to protect homesteaders, had been abandoned by the Army for active use when the Fourth Infantry was transferred to Alaska in May 1940. Only a maintenance detail of fifty men remained. The Army agreed

466 Italian Seamen to Be Interned Here

Justice Department Confirms Borrowing Of Fort at Missoula

Washington, April 12.—(AP)—The Justice department said today that 466 crew members of the Italian liner Conte Biancamano would be housed at Fort Missoula, Montana, one of two Army camps being borrowed by the Immigration service as supplementary quarters for persons held in deportation proceedings.

A second camp—Fort Lincoln, at Bismarck, N. D.—will be used to house crews of other Italian ships seized by the government to stop sabotage. In addition, 60 German seamen from two seized ships may be sent there.

The Italian government, the Justice department said, "has agreed to the quartering of these men at Fort Missoula."

Each camp contains barracks to house from 800 to 1,000 men and has hospital and recreation facilities. Men quartered in the camps, the department said, will be "under effective discipline and adequate guard."

About 1,300 Italian seamen are in custody.

Immigration service officials said a check of the number under indictment for sabotage had not been made and investigation of charges against some were still under way. They added that percentages of indictments were "very low," and cited as an example indictment of only nine of the 475 officers and men of the liner Conte Biancamano.

Those under indictment will be retained in the court districts in which they are indicted. Others sent to the internment camps will be transported by train at government expense under guard of border patrol officers. Departure dates have not been set.

All of the first group ordered to the camps will be sent to Missoula, the service said. Arrangements for moving the Civilian Conservation corps contingent from Fort Lincoln have been completed and officials were unable to say when the first seamen would be sent there.

AWAITING INFORMATION.

Colonel A. V. Ednie, commandant at Fort Missoula, when informed Saturday evening of the Justice department's announcement that 466 Italians will be housed at Fort Missoula, said that no official word in regard to the Fascist seamen has been received at the post as yet.

---

to transfer control of the camp to the Immigration and Naturalization Service for five years.[7] The INS, which fell under the jurisdiction of the Justice Department, assumed responsibility for the alien seamen.

In contrast to the stark settings of many of the internment camps that were to be established the following year, Fort Missoula was nestled in a scenic, lush valley. As one man detained at the fort was to describe the setting:

"To the southwest was a mountain range. To the east were battlefields where, it is said, the Bitterroot River which ran next to it ran red with blood during the Indian wars. Now there was fish in the clear cold water which flowed from the mountains which were still covered with snow. Wild flowers carpeted the fields, and there were even some purple iris bordering the barracks planted by someone who had lived there earlier. It was a quiet, beautiful place."[8]

That quiet, beautiful place came alive with the sounds of activity beginning in mid-April 1941 as the Immigration Service worked feverishly to prepare the camp for the arrival of a thousand seamen. It was a huge task that fell to Nick Collaer, an Immigration Service officer from Texas who was named supervisor of alien detentions at Missoula. There were several existing buildings on the grounds, but many had to be adapted for the special needs of the detainees. The Immigration Service required the following at the camp:

· Headquarters building
· Barracks, housing forty to sixty men, with a minimum of forty square feet of floor space for each man
· Warehouses for storage of equipment, supplies, food and baggage of the detainees

In mid-April 1941, Missoulians got their first word that the former U.S. Army camp at Fort Missoula would be home to Italian seamen.

Construction of new barracks began at Fort Missoula in 1941. The capacity reached 3,000, more than enough to accommodate the 1,000 Italians sent to Fort Missoula in May and 1,000 more Japanese who would arrive late in 1941 and in early 1942. The detention camp would be located just north of the quartermaster stable, foreground, and south of the site of the present Historical Museum. The officers' row houses, at right center, were torn down after the war.

MANSFIELD LIBRARY COLLECTION, UNIVERSITY OF MONTANA

Above
Facilities at Fort Missoula included a headquarters building in which the Immigration and Naturalization Service would be located. Behind it was a supply and office building and in the upper right is the recreation center.

Facing page
The fort also had a motor pool building that also served as a fire station.

• Commissary from which clothing, food and other articles are issued;
• Canteen for the sale to the detainees of articles that are not part of regular government issue
• Hospital that includes wards, private rooms, surgical space, an outpatient clinic, supply rooms, kitchen and an area for dental work
• Auditorium
• Guardhouse
• Firehouse
• Machine shop for repair of government vehicles and mechanical equipment
• Carpentry, plumbing and electrical shops
• Garage for storage of vehicles
• Fence and guard towers. The fence had to be an eight-foot, chainlink enclosure topped by barbed wire and illuminated by floodlights at night. The outer area was to remain darkened at night to permit guards to patrol without being seen from inside the camp.[9]

There were already four large dormitories that could accommodate one thousand men, but the Italian ships' officers demanded separate quarters and eating facilities.[10] Collaer could not obtain all the necessary supplies in time for the men's arrival, so he borrowed cots, mats and bedding from the U.S. Forest Service and the Civilian Conservation Corps and obtained $26,000 in medical and dental supplies from CCC camps in the Pacific Northwest.[11] Repairs to the post hospital, damaged in a recent fire, cost $26,000 and were incomplete upon the arrival of the Italians, necessitating the establishment of a temporary sick bay in one of the dormitories.

A recreation hall had only recently been completed for a CCC camp that had been housed at the fort and in it were a basketball court, bowling alleys, a dance hall, cocktail lounge and restaurant. [12]

A staff had to be assembled on short notice. It included a supervisor of alien detention, a chief patrol inspector, a chief surveillance officer responsible for outside surveillance of the camp, a chief liaison officer in charge of work details and all communication between the detainees and the chief supervisor, a chief supply officer, stewards, censors, interpreters and translators, a clerical staff, a surveillance division that had three officers of the watch and twenty-one patrol inspectors, a maintenance division that included a supervisor of construction and maintenance, a motor mechanic and four laborers, and a communications center staff. [13]

On April 14, 1941, Missoulians got their first look at the men who were to become their neighbors for the next two-and-one-half years. A page-one picture in the daily *Missoulian* showed five hundred Italian seamen disembarking from the U.S. Army transport ship *Leonard Wood*, which had picked them up in the Panama Canal Zone. Awaiting them at the pier in New York City were forty military policemen.

These seamen came from the *Conte Biancamano*, a cruise ship for the Lloyd Trestine Company of Trieste, Italy. Umberto Benedetti, one of 512 employees on the *Biancamano*, said the ship operated like a small city. There were saleswomen, waitresses, doctors, nurses, pharmacists, a priest, choreographers and dancers, entertainers, artists and sports teams on its staff. No one was hired to work on the *Biancamano* who did not have some special talent, including the ability to speak several languages. [14]

The ship's 45-day cruises took it along the Oriental route that included ports of call in Genoa, Gibralter, Singapore, Hong Kong, Shanghai and Manila. But in 1939 the ship took a different route, headed this time for Central America. Returning from Valparaiso, Benedetti recalls the ship was "trapped first at Balboa and second in the Panama Canal Zone. . . ."

The Fort Missoula Recreation Center, which opened in 1940, was built by Works Progress Administration and Civilian Conservation Corps crews. Its architect, Robert Reamer, also designed Yellowstone Park's Old Faithful Inn. The air-conditioned center included a basketball court, bowling alleys, boxing ring, stage, kitchen and bar. It was destroyed by fire on Dec. 7, 1946.
BILL SHARP COLLECTION

After languishing in port for 18 months, the men were transported to Ellis Island, their first stop on a trip that would take them to Fort Missoula.

The immigration service flew some of the ship's officers to Missoula in early May to permit them to consult with Collaer about the crew's accommodations and the camp's operation. Second officer Francesco La Rosa and purser Alssandro de Luca had nothing but praise for their treatment and their accommodations.

"How do you like Missoula?" they were asked.

"Very much, and you may tell the Chamber of Commerce here that we do."[15]

After a three-day trip on a train with the windows enclosed by bars, 135 seamen arrived in Missoula at 5:40 a.m. on May 9. Missoulians were warned not to gather at the point near the Buckhouse Bridge where the men would disembark from the cars that were diverted to a railroad spur line.[16] All roads leading to the unloading point were blocked and guarded by sheriff's deputies, border patrol guards and highway patrolmen. Only a day earlier the fence enclosing the fort was completed. On this day the iron gate at the entrance to the fort was closed.[17]

On the afternoon of the Italians' arrival, the *Missoula Sentinel* published a picture of some of them waving from the back of an Army truck. "One hundred twenty-five grinning, chattering Italian seamen sent from Ellis Island for internment at Fort Missoula, arrived early this morning, cheerfully accepting the post as their home for the duration of the war," the cutline read. An accompanying story told of their happiness at being in Missoula. "Che bella vista!" the men proclaimed as they disembarked. "What a beautiful sight." Bella Vista was from that day on the name that stuck.[18]

Italian Seamen Arrive Here for Internment

Fort Barracks Taken Over by Alien Throng

One hundred and twenty-three Italian seamen and 12 officers, from the luxury liner Conte Biancamano and other ships, pulled into Missoula at 5:40 o'clock this morning in their barred special train, stopped long enough for trainmen's orders and a whistle blast, then rolled on over the south spur to a designated point south of Fort Missoula, new detention station, where they were loaded into waiting Army trucks and whisked to barracks formerly occupied by soldiers at the post.

The scene of transfer from train to trucks and patrol cars was one of complete order and discipline. Alessandro De Luca and Francesco La Rosa, purser and second officer from the Conte Biancamano, were shouting orders to the men as they alighted from the train.

CITY CALLED BELLA VISTA BY ITALIANS

BY NICK MARIANA.

Three spoken words and a city is born.

Thus early this morning, as the sun climbed over Hell Gate's mountains, a special train carrying 125 Italian seamen came to a stop at an unloading point south of Fort Missoula, and among the first exclamations was:

"Che bella vista!"—(what a beautiful sight!)—and thus was a new city born. For now these Italian seamen have taken to their new location and are living in the city of, as they say, "Bella Vista."

Though somewhat amazed at the vastness of the United States and Montana, the men settled into the routine life at the Fort Missoula detention camp without displeasure. They seemed to enjoy being there. Their breakfast this morning was a complete one. They ate, showing a great liking for American food—especially butter and toast—which they consumed in large quantities.

They were unshaven, lightly dressed in civilian clothes. Some wore the typical Italian seamen's beret. They joked. They laughed. All were anxious to

The *Missoula Sentinel* recorded the arrival of the first seamen on May 9, 1941. They christened the camp "Bella Vista," meaning Beautiful Sight.

ITALIAN SEAMEN REACH INTERNMENT BASE HERE

One hundred twenty-five grinning, chattering Italian seamen, sent from Ellis island for internment at Fort Missoula, arrived early this morning, cheerfully accepting the post as their home for the duration of the war. The men, glad to reach their destination after a three-day railroad trip from the East, gave the Fascist salute when hailed by the Sentinel's photographer. This picture was taken as the Italians were loaded into trucks for the ride from the railroad spur near the fort to the military reservation. Uniformed man at left is an officer of the U. S. Border patrol. U. S. highway No. 93 was blocked until the procession of trucks full of interned sailors had passed.

The seamen were moved from the train to Army transport trucks for the brief trip to the fort in what was described as a scene of "complete order and discipline." Three of the sailors had dogs with them; several brought musical instruments. Once at the fort there was roll call, followed by a breakfast that included "lots of butter and toast." Some of the men even put butter in their coffee.[19]

The Italian consul at Seattle arrived the next day to confer with the *Biancamano* crew. Antonio Tosconi Millo told the men:

"As Italy's representative from the Italian consulate at Seattle I must ask you to set an example of behavior that typifies our great country. Your behavior must be such that the guards will not have the slightest necessity to ask questions. Remember that you must remain within the confines of the iron fence."[20]

Millo wanted the Missoula townspeople to know that the Italian government was pleased that the seamen were being housed at the fort until their passage home could be arranged. The next day he told the *Missoulian*: "Our seamen are very fortunate indeed to have such a wonderful location at Fort Missoula for their detention station. The climate is ideal and everyone is being so very nice to them." Millo said the men's needs were being taken care of and they especially enjoyed the food, prepared by American and Italian cooks "working side by side in the kitchen."[21] Millo and his companion, Guiseppe Bovio, a cultural attache from the Seattle consulate, were on their way to conduct business with Pietro Maria Amabile, head of the Italian consulate in Butte.

The train that brought the seamen from Ellis Island made several trips. On May 20, an additional 483 men arrived, including a doctor, priest, recreation leaders, a band and an orchestra.[22] Joining the sailors and *Biancamano* crew were 62 Italians who had come to the United States to work

at the Italian pavilion at the 1939 World's Fair in New York and were prevented by the war's outbreak from returning to Italy.[23] Several more Italians were brought to the fort and by mid-June the population had reached 868. The men were not unhappy with their lives at "Bella Vista," but theirs was not an entirely satisfying existence either, for there was little to occupy their days.

"'Si mangia, si veve e si dorme—e questro e la vita a Bella Vista.'

"(We eat, we drink and we sleep and this is the life at Bella Vista.)

"That's what 800-odd Italian seamen interned at Fort Missoula detention station, which the Italians have named Bella Vista, will say when you ask how they like being interned.

"And it isn't the life of Riley."[24]

Reporter Nick Mariana went on to describe in the June 15 *Missoulian* story a typical day at the fort: The men arise anywhere from 7 to 9 a.m., eat in shifts apart from the officers, who have their own eating facilities. Many take walks around the camp, then either head back to their bunks or rest in the cool grass. The walk around the camp perimeter is a distance of two thousand yards, past 60-foot guard towers at the north and south gates and twelve guards constantly on patrol.

"Patrol guards roll around at regular intervals and a stringent check system is in operation at the post gate and also at the high iron gates and fences of confinement," Mariana reported. The barracks, which housed about fifty men each, are crowded with double bunks, permitting the men barely enough room to slip from the upper bunks to the floor. The Immigration Service was building the foundations for thirteen additional prefabricated bunkhouses.

Many seamen spent their free time building elaborate ship miniatures.
PICTORIAL HISTORIES COLLECTION

Some seamen passed the time by doing handiwork. Ship miniatures were displayed everywhere. Men engaged in frequent games of soccer or bocce. Letter writing was a popular pastime. Mariana described one scene in which a photographer for the newspaper began to take pictures:

"Photographia, qui! Fa mi una photographia." (Make me a picture.)

Italians Lucky To Be at Fort Says A. T. Millo

Official of Consulate at Seattle Asserts Climate Is Ideal for Men.

"Our seamen are very fortunate indeed to have such a wonderful location at Fort Missoula for their detention station. The climate is ideal, and everyone is being so very nice to them," said Antonio Toscani Millo, Italian consul from Seattle, and his companion, Guiseppe Bovio, cultural attache, before leaving for Butte Sunday morning.

Mr. Millo and Mr. Bovio left Sunday to take up official business with the consulate at Butte. The two Italian officials returned to the city late Sunday to confer with Chief Immigration Inspector N. D. Colaer and Preston R. McLaughlin, chief inspector of the border patrol.

Saturday afternoon, Mr. Millo spoke to the Italian seamen being held at the Fort Missoula detention station, explaining the necessity of "good behavior."

Men Ask No More.

In a statement late Saturday night, Mr. Millo said that he did not know how long his government wished him to stay here. The wants of the detained men are being taken care of, and Mr. Millo said that the American food being served at the station is greatly enjoyed by the Italians.

"American and Italian cooks are working side by side in the kitchens, and the food is excellent," he said.

Mr. Millo has been with the Italian consulate at Seattle for the past three years, and has been in the United States since 1935.

Pietro Maria Amabile Notti, head of the Italian consulate at Butte, has resigned his position because of ill health, Mr. Millo said on his return here Sunday evening.

Officials from the Italian consulate in Seattle visited Fort Missoula to check conditions and told a *Missoulian* reporter that they were pleased with what they found.

"They wanted pictures of themselves to send home to let loved ones know how well they were. Individual photographing is prohibited, but how they pile into group pictures."

"Life at the fort was pleasant," they told Mariana. "But how wonderful it would be if we could have our families, here even for a few days," they said.

Not surprisingly, music was an integral part of the life at Bella Vista, given the number of musicians from both the World's Fair and the *Conte Biancamano*. After a 5 p.m. supper, musical performances were a nightly affair. A band played in one part of the camp while the audience sang Italian songs. "In other parts of the camp an orchestra puts on a concert of its own and in still other rooms of the barracks, violinists, pianists and other musical instruments can be heard. This is their night life," Mariana reported.

While the men "chatted continually about life at the camp, their hobbies, the music, the food," they would not talk about the war, he told his readers.

Umberto Benedetti remembers life at the camp fondly. A typical day, he recalls, consisted of tennis, soccer, swimming, dancing or listening to music or opera. "The life was just like an ordinary life, just like now," he said.[25]

Religion appeared to be central to the life at the fort. Benedetti built an altar that was used during church services by an Italian priest, the Rev. Bruno, a chaplain on the *Biancamano* who was detained at the fort. Benedetti said Archbishop Amleto Cicognano of Washington, D.C., even visited the Italian men at the fort and said Mass. The *Missoulian* noted that the seamen were quite religious and Mariana reported that when services were held each Sunday "everyone goes."[26]

But that religious fervor either was overestimated or just did not endure. Some time later—the date is not clear—Rev. Bruno complained to officials in charge that the men were becoming increasingly lax in attending Mass. The authorities arranged a solution. Weekly rations of tobacco had been given to the men each Sunday as they left the barracks to attend Mass. Many were taking the tobacco and returning to their bunks. The authorities changed that practice after the complaint from the priest and handed out the tobacco only as the men left the church. "Attendance from then on was 100 percent," a camp official reported.[27]

Discipline problems were quite minor in the early months of the Italians' stay at Fort Missoula, however. The seamen seemed to resign themselves to confinement at the fort and spent the late spring and summer of 1941 getting accustomed to this new life, uncertain of their future and unable to anticipate the length of this sojourn in Missoula.

The camp was enclosed by a fence and 60-foot guard towers stood at the north and south gates.
MANSFIELD LIBRARY COLLECTION, UNIVERSITY OF MONTANA

Among the Italians detained at the fort was Umberto Benedetti, front row, far left. Like many other Italians at the fort, Benedetti worked on the Italian cruise ship *Conte Biancamano*, which was docked in a U.S. port when World War II broke out in Europe. UMBERTO BENEDETTI COLLECTION

Unrest from Inside and Outside the Camp

By mid-July 1941 nearly a thousand Italians lived at Fort Missoula. It was a quiet, routine existence that many would come to find intolerably boring, but as one man remarked, it was better than going home to a country embroiled in war.[1] Two incidents interrupted the peaceful life of the men at Fort Missoula. One instigator of unrest came from inside the camp, the other from thousands of miles away.

There were both fascists and anti-fascists among the ranks of men interned at the fort. One account put the number of pro-fascists at the fort at 250, among them journalists and active members of pro-fascist organizations in the United States, and others detained "simply because there was some reason to suspect that their loyalty to Fascist Italy might be stronger than their loyalty to the American government."[2] Some of these men had sons who were fighting in the American army and many of those detained were bitter about it.

"Six hundred thousand Italian aliens in this country get the Attorney General's blessings for being good Americans—and they had to pick on me," one of the men told a camp visitor. "So what if I did write in a newspaper that I thought Mussolini was doing a good job? Does that make me a Fascist? I was finished with that son of a bitch as soon as he teamed up with that other son of a bitch in Germany, but I can't get that through the skulls of those people in the Attorney General's office."[3]

Political discord between the two groups was held at bay most of the time but one crisis precipitated by political tensions erupted just over a year after the men had arrived at the fort. The instigator, oddly enough, was an American medical doctor assigned to the fort hospital. Dr. Orvall Smiley was apparently a man who had difficulty getting along with just about anyone. Nick Collaer, the camp supervisor, reported to immigration authorities that Smiley was involved in disagreements with the detainees, nurses, other doctors and patrol guards.[4]

Smiley's disagreeable temperament, which Collaer characterized initially as a lack of tact, caused what was the only serious political conflict among the Italians.

Former University of Montana student Susan Buchel, who wrote a paper about the Italians' experiences at Fort Missoula, recounted the events from Immigration Service investigation reports this way:

"On September 3, 1942, a riot flamed at the camp between fascists and antifascist detainees. Dr. Smiley had sparked the fight by very foolishly posting a letter written to him by one of the anti-fascists containing matter offensive to one of the fascists. One of the detainees assaulted the writer of the letter, after which several detainees searched out and attacked a small number of other anti-fascists. The fighting spread quickly over the camp,

Facing page
A mounted Immigration and Naturalization Service guard patrols outside the camp along the Bitterroot River.
MONTANA HISTORICAL SOCIETY COLLECTION

involving many men. An emergency squad of guards entered and used a canister of gas to disburse the group, taking thirteen detainees into custody. Five men had been injured seriously enough to require hospitalization."[5]

This incident was an isolated one, as life at the fort was generally harmonious, especially for the seamen. Most were cheerful and while many weren't happy to be confined—some even complaining that their lives separated from women was a breach of the Geneva Convention's proscription against cruel and inhuman treatment—they accepted the circumstances that brought them to Missoula.[6]

There was one attempt from the outside to sow seeds of discontent and it got international notice.

Armando Tosi, manager of the Italian restaurant at the New York World's Fair, was able to secure passage to Italy in 1941. Once home, he gave interviews in the Italian press—which were picked up by newspapers in the United States—in which he characterized the treatment of the detained Italians as "bestial."[7] Tosi claimed Americans were so fearful of fifth column activity that Italians and Germans in the United States were being arrested "indiscriminately on the flimsiest pretexts and treated as common criminals." He said the Italians housed in a "concentration camp" at Fort Missoula were "watched by policemen, the majority of whom are Jews," and were kept in jail "with the scum of American criminals."[8]

Concerned that the report would cause consternation in the Italian-American community, *Il Progresso* and *Corriere D'America,* Italian-language newspapers published in New York City, sent reporters to Missoula to investigate the claims. *Corriere D'America* printed pages of photographs of the camp and its inhabitants and "found no spirit of a concentration camp or prison camp,"[9] while *Il Progresso*'s reporter found "10,000 acres of land with all the characteristics of a summer resort."[10] Only a handful of guards patrolled the camp and no machine guns were in evidence, the *New York Times* quoted *Il Progresso* as reporting.

Time magazine also sent a reporter to the camp. "The detainees (never referred to as prisoners) govern themselves, spend their time reading, listening to the radio, playing games, doing chores for pin money," the magazine reported. "They are not forced to work."[11]

The fascist government in Italy joined the attack on the United States for the detention of its seamen, though it had agreed in early May 1941 that housing the men at the fort was an acceptable plan. When an American consular clerk in Italy was inexplicably detained for four days in a San Vittore prison, fascist officials refused to tell the American government why he was arrested. Italian authorities said the arrest of Raymond Hall involved a "single private citizen" while in the United States "several dozen Italian citizens were arrested and sent to prison" for "acts which did no harm to the United States."[12]

The inhabitants of the fort, now numbering 1,056 with the arrival of sixty-four men on August 18, had few complaints about their treatment. Any grievances they did express were handled through a governing body created by the men themselves, at the urging of Nick Collaer. There was a general council of twenty-eight, selected by the men, that included a mayor, police chief, parks commissioner and sanitary commissioner.

The mayor was the spokesman for the entire group in its communications with camp officials.[13]

The men were provided food, clothing and medical and dental care without cost to them.[14] It wasn't always easy to secure good medical care, however. Chief Medical Officer Frank Brown complained to Immigration Service officials about the problem he encountered getting eye doctors:

"In the last six months we have had four different eye specialists. Eye examinations have been a constant source of trouble for me, principally because the eye specialists are so busy with their own practices that they do not seem to be interested in our work. In addition to this, the language incompatibility, neuroses and unreasonable requests made to these doctors by the detainees makes it possible for me to understand their lack of interest in our work.

"Two days ago I contacted our new eye specialist, Dr. Marshall. On informing him that he had our contract, the first thing he said was that he was sorry he had bid on it in the first place. So you can see we are more or less at their mercy."[15]

The budget for the camp in fiscal year 1942 was projected by Collaer at $389,800. It provided forty cents per day, per man for food, five cents a day for clothing, two cents a day for laundry, two cents per day for hospitalization and dentistry costs, and close to $90,000 for the year for general supplies, utilities, repairs and maintenance.[16] Actual costs fluctuated somewhat, and by early Fall of 1941 Collaer projected the daily cost per man at 65 cents. That included 34 cents a day to feed each person.[17]

The food was plentiful, and by most accounts, good, though at first several Italians complained about the heavy reliance on canned foods, which

The men were assigned chores at the camp. This is the Italian kitchen crew.
MANSFIELD LIBRARY COLLECTION, UNIVERSITY OF MONTANA

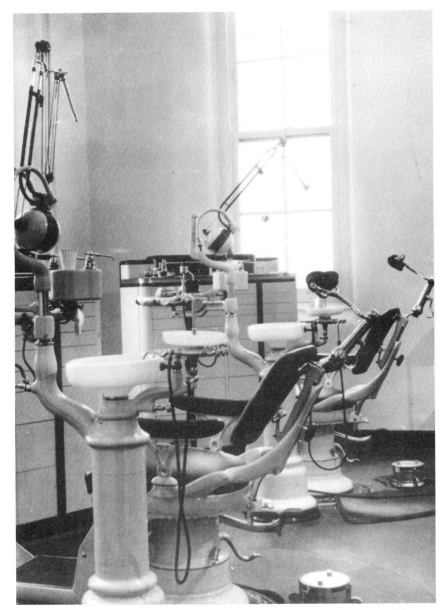

they considered poisonous.[18] Some of the supplies were purchased from a Missoula grocery, D'Orazi's. Ann D'Orazi, who was in 1943 to marry Alfredo Cipolato, an Italian detained at the fort, said her father delivered groceries to Fort Missoula for the Immigration Service. Ironically, the men were able to get supplies that were strictly rationed for Americans.

Ann Cipolato recalls: "They got sugar, they got oil, they got anything they wanted [such as] coffee. Anything they wanted, my dad would get a permit and would try and get it and they got it." Alfredo Cipolato agrees that the men at the fort ate better than many Missoulians.[19] Border patrolman Lyle Slade said the Italians were fed round steak at a time he was unable to get even hamburger.[20]

The Italians got food that was strictly rationed for Americans. This detainee surveys his Christmas dinner.
MONTANA HISTORICAL SOCIETY COLLECTION

The Italians ate in a large mess hall. Portraits of Benito Mussolini and King Victor Emmanuel III lined one wall.
MONTANA HISTORICAL SOCIETY COLLECTION

Dramatic productions and musical performances entertained the detainees and townspeople invited to the events held on the Recreation Center stage.
MANSFIELD LIBRARY COLLECTION, UNIVERSITY OF MONTANA

The Italians did not get quite everything they wanted, however. No alcohol was permitted, but it was a ban the Italians worked hard to overcome. "We used to make our own but no alcohol [was] allowed," Cipolato said. "Dried raisin, dried prune, dry apricots, dry anything—dry figs. We used to get all these dry food for dessert but we used to save them."[21]

Though the first summer at the fort was uneventful for the men, the compound was the site of constant activity as the government prepared the fort to handle additional detainees. In early July, thirty-two barracks were under construction as part of a plan to increase the capacity of the fort to two thousand, about double the present population. Just a few weeks after that construction began, the Immigration Service announced plans for another sixteen barracks, bringing the capacity of the fort to three thousand.[22] For some reason, those sixteen barracks were never built because the capacity of the fort was never listed as greater than two thousand.

By late summer the Italians began to interact with the Missoula community on a limited basis. In early August a trio that had performed at the World's Fair played for a Missoula service club. The pianist, cellist and violinist were said to be among Italy's finest musicians. On August 14 a public concert was presented at Fort Missoula, featuring a string quintet. The group's musical director and pianist was Dante Dall'Aglio, a former conductor of the Diana Rovigo Theater in Milan and a graduate of the University of Parma. Corrado Guizzari, on first violin, had studied at the University of Genoa, as had Gaetano Gambetti, the cellist. Since 1930 all four had played on the most important ocean liners of the Italian

Mealtime at the Italian mess hall, 1942. MONTANA HISTORICAL SOCIETY

The men frequently took both male and female roles for the plays performed at Fort Missoula. Seated at lower right is Umberto Benedetti, who remained in Missoula after the war.
UMBERTO BENEDETTI COLLECTION

Facing page
This playbill is from *Sly*, a drama in three parts that was performed at Fort Missoula on May 17, 1942.
UMBERTO BENEDETTI COLLECTION

and Societa Trestine steamship lines.[23] Collaer said the men were among the more than one hundred musicians and entertainers at the fort.[24]

The Italians held regular concerts, charging a small admission price. They engendered good will among the Missoula community not only by producing musical events, but also by voting to contribute ten percent of their proceeds from one concert to the Missoula Iron Lung Foundation.[25] They also performed plays frequently, including several in which the men played both male and female parts. One such play was "Romanticismo," a drama in four acts that featured eighteen actors.[26] Among others were "I Pirati," a play with twenty-three actors and an orchestra of thirteen, and a three-act drama, "Sly."[27]

Though Missoulians were allowed on the fort grounds only infrequently for camp productions, Collaer kept townspeople informed of the goings-on at the camp through his frequent speeches to service clubs. About half of the Italians spoke some English, he reported, while others spoke Spanish or French and some were fluent in many languages. Collaer reminded one group to keep in mind that the men are "not common criminals and that no criminal problem is involved." He said his job was to "keep up morale" and provide clothing and entertainment.[28] "None seem to harbor any ill feelings toward America," he said. "One detainee went so far as to say he would crawl ten miles on his hands and knees to kiss the American flag if he could become an American citizen." Collaer characterized the men as "homeloving,

★ ★ ★ ★ ★ ★ ★

C A M P O   F O R T   M I S S O U L A
DOMENICA 17 MAGGIO 1942 XX ·· ORE 20
------o------

D. I. M. M.

Il Gruppo Filodrammatico diretto dal camerata CESARE GUIDI

Presenta :

S L Y

O V V E R O

LA LEGGENDA DEL DORMIENTE RISVEGLIATO

Dramma in 3 atti di Gioacchino Forzano

P E R S O N A G G I

Sly	camerata	CESARE GUIDI
Dolly	"	NATALE VERARDO
Il Conte	"	MARIO BERGAMINI
John Plake	"	GUSTAVO MASULLO
Ostessa	"	PIETRO ANTOLA
Un nobile	"	GIUSEPPE MARCHESE
Altro nobile	"	CARLO MANGINI
Servo del conte	"	GIUSEPPE FABRIS
Beone	"	ALFREDO CIPOLATO
Beone	"	GIUSEPPE DELLEPIANE
Il gobbo	"	EMILIO NERI
Giocatore di scacchi	"	MASSIMO NARDINI
Un baro	"	SALVATORE BARRESI
Un avventore	"	ROMEO SANTUCCI
Snare, l'agente dello Sceriffo	"	UMBERTO PRINA
Ancella	"	GEROLAMO REBORA
Ancella	"	EZIO MARIOTTO
Un paggio	"	RAIMONDO VISCIANO
Un violino	"	GIOVANNI ROSSI
Un musico	"	ALFIO LUPI
Un vecchio servo	"	GUSTAVO MASULLO
Suonatori della taverna	"	ROCCA — BEZZI — PRANDO

--o°o°--

Buttafuori············camerata CESARE GRAZIANI

Scenario del camerata RAUL BANZI
in collaborazione col camerata LIONELLO DE MARCHIS

Attrezzatura scenica UMBERTO BENEDETTI
············

Abbigliamenti a cura del camerata ERCOLE SILVA

NELLA SALA E ASSOLUTAMENTE VIETATO FUMARE

★ ★ ★ ★ ★ ★

regular people" who caused little trouble and had not attempted to escape from the compound. The men are content, morale is good and Bella Vista "is just another thriving little community," he said.[29]

Though assurances that the men were harmless were regularly given to the community, security at the fort was nonetheless uniformly tight. No one was allowed onto the grounds without first registering at one of the two main gates. Armed guards patrolled outside the fence that surrounded the camp and also stood watch in towers at each corner of the compound. A communications system linked the guard towers to the central office.[30]

The immigration service established rules for the daily routine. Reveille was at six, followed by breakfast in shifts. One man from each of the tables of ten was assigned to serve the food from the kitchen. Washroom facilities were available after breakfast. Roll call was daily at 8 a.m. and 8 p.m. Duties were rotated among the groups, though the jobs were not taxing. The men were expected to perform, without pay, work that was necessary to the general operation of the camp. If they did specialized tasks, such as carpentry, blacksmithing, or machinist's work, they were paid 80 cents a day. Paid projects encouraged by the Immigration Service included mattress making, sewing, furniture making, rug weaving, construction, and laying of sidewalks and roads.[31]

Outside the work day, in addition to musical and dramatic productions, the men engaged in sports like soccer and were encouraged to take up arts and crafts. Not all of the detainees embraced these leisure activities. A camp visitor admired a landscape painting of one Italian who had been brought to the fort for his pro-fascist activities.

"I see you're an artist as well as a journalist," the visitor said.

He laughed but there was no mirth in his laughter. "I never painted a goddamn thing in my life until I got to this place. It was the fucking FBI that made an artist out of me."[32]

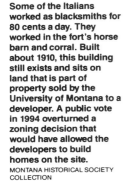

Some of the Italians worked as blacksmiths for 80 cents a day. They worked in the fort's horse barn and corral. Built about 1910, this building still exists and sits on land that is part of property sold by the University of Montana to a developer. A public vote in 1994 overturned a zoning decision that would have allowed the developers to build homes on the site.
MONTANA HISTORICAL SOCIETY COLLECTION

Routine chores, like laundry duty, were expected to be done as part of the men's keep. These chores were rotated among all the men. Entrance to the tailor and laundry shop was restricted to the men who worked there. MONTANA HISTORICAL SOCIETY COLLECTION

The men were permitted to send and receive letters, but the mail was censored. This letter was sent to Tommaso Santori. It passed through the neutral port of Lisbon, Portugal, then through New York. It was stamped, "Detained Alien Enemy Mail."

At least one of the Italians whose family lived in America was also unhappy over how his family viewed his predicament. A question about what he was doing in the camp brought this exchange:

" 'I'm here because I'm unlucky. I've always been unlucky. I'm even unlucky about my children.' He showed me a letter he had recently received from a daughter in Detroit named Gladys. 'Dear Dad,' it read. 'I was sorry to hear of your detention. I wouldn't worry about it though. You being an Italian and unnaturalized has put you in an enemy classification. But there is no need to worry as long as you have done nothing. There is great satisfaction in knowing that Uncle Sam is on the job, isn't there? I'm just tickled pink they aren't letting anything slip past them. I do hope you will be out soon though.'

" 'She takes after her mother,' he grumbled. 'A woman with the brain of a cretina.'

"The man had been detained because he had in his possession two contraband items, a shortwave radio and a Graflex camera. He was also reportedly overhead to say he believed that one day Hitler would conquer the world. His file characterized him as 'as dangerous an alien enemy as could be found in the United States,' but after a review by the U.S. Attorney General's office, the man was released."[33]

Though the camp officials tried to provide outlets for relaxation, the boredom of the daily routine was to take its toll. In a report to the Immigration Service, the camp medical officer noted that in one month there were 1,404 sick calls recorded from among only 1,227 men. "This is directly attributed to the fact that some of these men have been away from their homes and families for three or four years, incarcerated in prisons and detained in camps," officer Frank Brown reported. He said cases of "neurosis and other neurogenic illnesses" were increasing to "startling proportions."

"If these men are not furnished more work and liberties, I dread to think what the conditions will be one year from now," he said.[34]

Any hope that the men had of a quick return to their homeland was dashed in December 1941 when, in the wake of the attack at Pearl Harbor and the United States' declaration of war with Japan, Germany and Italy declared war on the United States.

The Italians at the fort refused to discuss the state of war with a reporter sent to inquire about their reaction. One camp official told the *Missoulian* there was "less excitement among the Italians about the declaration of war than there was on he streets of Missoula." The newspaper said the routine at the fort remained unchanged by the turn of events.

"Closing of the gate at the intersection of South and Reserve Avenues, blocking the front entrance to the Fort Missoula alien detention station, was the only outward sign Thursday that the United States had gone to war with the motherland of the 1,100 Italians who are being held."[35]

The only difference was that these sailors, musicians, entertainers and chefs were now "enemy aliens." Soon they would be joined by other men, all of whom the United States government had classified as enemies.

THE ROOTS OF PREJUDICE

THE UNITED STATES' entry into the war, precipitated by the attack by Japanese forces at Pearl Harbor, was to secure Missoula a significant but little-known niche in history. Beginning in the days following that attack and continuing for almost six months, Fort Missoula would house nearly a thousand men whom the United States government considered its most insidious enemies on American soil.

Hundreds of Japanese men living on the west coast of the United States were rounded up beginning December 7 and sent to Missoula. Who were these men, taken from their homes, stripped of all but their most essential possessions, separated from their families, their livelihoods irrevocably interrupted? What had they done? In many cases they were the leaders of the Japanese community in America and their "crime" was their success.

Anti-Japanese sentiment had been simmering in the United States since before the turn of the century. It most frequently came to a boil in California, where Oriental exclusion laws had their genesis and where racist organizations flourished with the help of the Hearst media syndicate. The "yellow peril" fears sprang from misconceptions about the Japanese birth rate, their failure to assimilate into the American "melting pot," their religious affiliations, separate Japanese-language schools, industrious work habits and their practice of retaining Japanese citizenship even after years of residence in America. Nearly all of these fears were either groundless or were the consequences of racial prejudices in the United States that took the form of legislation barring the Japanese from the usual freedoms and privileges accorded Caucasians.

The Commission on Wartime Relocation and Internment of Civilians, established by Congress in 1980 to review America's World War II relocation and internment program and to recommend remedies for any wrongs done by the United States government, explained the roots of the Japanese exclusion in its report, *Personal Justice Denied*:

"The Japanese immigrants were excluded from political life by the prohibition against naturalization and were effectively barred from participation in social and economic affairs. As with many new immigrant groups, they brought with them customs and mores which also tended to set them apart in the early years after arrival. There was a sustaining pride in the Japanese people and its culture, which honored social values and cohesive group relationships, with particular deference to those in positions of authority and status within the family and community. These factors promoted internal solidarity within the Japanese community and, combined with the hostile nativism of California, placed the Issei (immigrant generation from Japan) in comparative isolation in the public and economic life of the West Coast."[1]

The notion that the Japanese and other Asians had an exceptionally high birth rate was commonplace. When the Alien Land Law of 1920 was being debated, the governor of California tried to prove that the Japanese birth rate was three times that of white residents of the state. Through misleading statistics he seemed to do just that, though in reality the birth rate of Japanese in America was below that of European immigrants. By 1940 it was lower than the birth rate of the general population of every state on the West Coast.[2] In addition to the mistaken notions about the birth rate, famine conditions in Asia early in the 20th century sparked rumors that waves of immigration to the United States from the Far East could be expected. In truth, at its peak in 1907 Japanese immigration to the United States was less than 3 percent of total immigration, and in California, where fears were most deep-seated, the Japanese population never reached more than 2.1 percent of the population.[3]

This xenophobia was entrenched in American culture and law almost from the birth of the nation. The Naturalization Act of 1790 limited citizenship to any "free white person." It was later amended to specifically prohibit citizenship for Chinese immigrants and in 1922 the Supreme Court interpreted the law to exclude all Asians from naturalization.[4] Ironically, one of the charges leveled against the Issei as America was pulled into World War II was that they were likely to be disloyal because they had not renounced their Japanese citizenship. Barred from United States citizenship, they had no other choice.

At a political rally in San Francisco in 1900, Mayor James Duval Phelan expressed an opinion that was pervasive on the West Coast: "The Japanese are starting the same tide of immigration which we thought we had checked twenty years ago. . . . The Chinese and Japanese are not bona fide citizens. They are not the stuff of which American citizens can be made. . . ."[5]

This kind of prejudice led not only to laws that barred Japanese from citizenship, but also to the 1913 Alien Land Law that prohibited those Japanese already in America from purchasing land, and limited agricultural leases to three years. The Japanese circumvented that law by placing the ownership of land in the names of their children, American-born Nisei who by the Fourteenth Amendment were guaranteed American citizenship. A 1920 law aimed to prevent that circumvention by prohibiting the Japanese from acting as guardians of their native-born children, but that was struck down by the courts.

Many Japanese tried to rear their children to live in either culture, fearing that one day they would be prohibited from living in the United States. As part of that pattern, some children attended Japanese-language schools after their regular school hours. In some of these schools the slant was undeniably pro-Japanese. U.S. Sen. Daniel Inouye of Hawaii recalled his language schooling:

"Day after day the (Buddhist) priest who taught us ethics and Japanese history hammered away at the divine prerogatives of the Emperor. . . . He would tilt his menacing crew-cut skull at us and solemnly proclaim, 'You must remember that only a trick of fate has brought you so far from your homeland, but there must be no question of your loyalty. When Japan calls, you must know that it is Japanese blood that flows in your veins.'"[6]

About half the Japanese in the United States were Buddhist and half Christian. A few were Shinto, which was less a religion than a patriotic worship of the emperor of Japan.

Nearly half of the immigrant Japanese were farmers. Their success was threatening to traditional farmers, who retaliated by pressing for alien land laws. In 1917 the average yield per acre among all California farmers brought fewer than $42; for the Issei the average income per acre was $141.[7] Though the Japanese in California occupied only one percent of the cultivated land in the state, by 1919 they were producing ten percent of the total value of California produce.[8] By 1920 the market value of crops produced by California Issei was $67 million. It was the same story in other coastal states. In Oregon by 1940 the Japanese were growing $2.7 million worth of produce, while in Washington the total reached $4 million a year.[9]

Those factors created an anti-Asian suspicion that pervaded all levels of society, both civilian and government. Evidence that the government was monitoring the actions of Japanese in the United States and contemplating their imprisonment in the event of war is evident in a memorandum sent by President Roosevelt to the chief of Naval Operations on August 10, 1936. Roosevelt had been advised that some Japanese living in Hawaii had regular contact with Japanese merchant ships docking in Oahu. He decided—five years before the attack at Pearl Harbor—that any Japanese who had contact with any of these merchant ships "should be secretly but definitely identified and his or her name placed on a special list of those who would be first to be placed in a concentration camp in the event of trouble."[10]

Three years later Roosevelt authorized the expansion of this surveillance to the mainland. He directed the Federal Bureau of Investigation, the Office of Naval Intelligence and the Army's G-2 branch to coordinate all espionage, counter-espionage and sabotage investigations. The FBI compiled a list of Japanese to watch and placed the suspects in one of three categories:

"A"—Known dangerous. These were people who were influential in the Japanese community or who because of their work were considered likely fifth-column agents. The list included fishermen, produce distributors, Shinto and Buddhist priests, farmers, influential businessmen, members of the Japanese consulate, or aliens who led cultural or assistance organizations. All had been investigated by agents.

"B"—Potentially dangerous. This list consisted of the people thought likely to be disloyal but who had not been thoroughly investigated.

"C"—People who demonstrated pro-Japanese inclinations or engaged in unspecified propaganda activities. This category included people who were members of, or gave money to, ethnic groups, or were Japanese language teachers, martial arts instructors, travel agents or newspaper editors.[11]

An intelligence report submitted to Roosevelt noted that it was "easy to get on the suspect list, merely a speech in favor of Japan at some banquet, being sufficient to land one there." Curtis Munson, a Chicago businessman who prepared the report at Roosevelt's behest after gathering information under the guise of a government official, said the intelli-

Above and facing page
The attack on Pearl Harbor on Dec. 7, 1941, prompted the Federal Bureau of Investigation to begin arresting Japanese living in the United States who the government feared might be allies of Japan. These "dangerous enemy aliens" were sent to Fort Missoula. The surprise attack left much of the Pacific fleet in ruins.

PICTORIAL HISTORIES COLLECTION

gence agencies "are generous with the title of suspect and are taking no chances."[12]

The government's official line was somewhat different. Immigration Service Commissioner Earl Harrison said that those on the suspect list who were subsequently arrested were enemy aliens who by their "activities, affiliations or relationships in enemy countries indicated potential or possible danger to our internal security."[13]

Munson said the Japanese were "hampered as saboteurs because of their easily recognized physical appearance" and the fact that few had access to important jobs or information that would aid the enemy. After acknowledging that there might be "the odd case of fanatical sabotage by some Japanese 'crackpot,' " Munson concluded: "For the most part the local Japanese are loyal to the United States or, at worst, hope that by remaining quiet they can avoid concentration camps or irresponsible mobs. We do not believe that they would be at least any more disloyal than any other racial group in the United States with whom we went to war."[14]

Nonetheless, one month from the date of that report, within hours of Japan's attack on an unprepared Pacific fleet at Pearl Harbor, the arrests of those on the "ABC" list began. Commissioner Harrison said later that "hysteria played no part" in choosing those who would be arrested. Many, he said, were distinctly hostile to the United States. Germans taken into custody and sent to Fort Stanton, New Mexico, or Fort Lincoln, North Dakota, were "admitted Nazis," while the Japanese, he said, left no doubt about their allegiance to Japan.[15]

Donald Nakahata's father was one of those arrested. Shiro Nakahata was a part-time newspaperman and a member of the Japanese Community Association in San Francisco.

"My father was arrested either December 7 or December 8," Nakahata recalled. "He was working for the Japanese association of San Francisco

and San Jose. After Pearl Harbor he figured that in San Francisco there would be enough community leaders, so that somebody needed to cover the Japanese community in San Jose. So he decided to go there. And I walked him to the bus stop. We went down Pine Street down to Fillmore to the number 22 streetcar, and he took the 22 streetcar and went to the SP (Southern Pacific) and took the train to San Jose. And that was the last time I saw him.

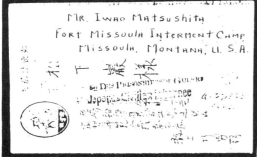

Form 1618
82085

Comité International de la Croix-Rouge
du Conseil General, GENEVE (Suisse)

AMERICAN RED CROSS
Washington, D. C.

EXAMINED
By 102

Civilian Message Form

SENDER — ENVOYER

Name — Nom   MATSUSHITA / 6659
Christian name — Prénom   IWAO
Street — Rue   FORT MISSOULA
City — Localité   MISSOULA
State — Province   MONTANA

Message to be transmitted — Message à transmettre —
(not more than 25 words, family news of strictly personal character.) (25 mots
au maximum, nouvelles de caractère strictement personnel et familial.)

SAFE AND SOUND IN CAMP. TREATED
KINDLY. MEALS OTHER ACCOMMODATIONS
GOOD. WIFE MOVING TO NEW
LOCATION.
REGARDS TO RELATIVES FRIENDS.
TAKE GOOD CARE ESPECIALLY MOTHER.

Chapter   Missoula County   Date 4/30/42

ADDRESSEE — DESTINATAIRE
CITIZENSHIP   JAPANESE
Name   MATSUSHITA   BIRTH — NAISSANCE
                                      Place   MIIKE, JAPAN
Christian name   SEKIO   and Date FEB. 22, 1890
                                                (Lieu et Date)
Street   KWANSEI GAKUIN   Citizen of   JAPAN
                              Name (MATSUSHITA, ISAO
                              of father)
Locality NISHINOMIYA   Relationship to inquirer BROTHER
Province   HYOGO-KEN   Country   JAPAN

Reply on the reverse side
Write very legibly   Réponse au verso
                                  Ecrire très lisiblement

The families of many Japanese men brought to Fort Missoula had no knowledge initially about where their husbands and fathers had been sent. After several weeks the men were permitted to correspond and these messages were sent to and received from Iwao Matsushita.

"And I guess that was the last time that anybody saw him in our family. Finally, word came through the grapevine somehow that the FBI had picked him up, and he was now being held at a detention station on Silver Avenue someplace in San Francisco."[16]

Nakahata said his mother bundled some clothes together for his father, but he had been moved by the time she got to the detention station. Nakahata does not know where his father was taken, though he recalls some mail came from Fort Sill, Oklahoma. Records at the National Archives show that Shiro T. Nakahata was sent to Fort Missoula and later in 1942 was transferred to Fort Sill. He died in camp.

"We got a telegram one night after dinner saying that he'd died and that we should advise the authorities by eight o'clock the following morning as to the disposition of the remains, or they would simply bury him in the cemetery there," his son said. "So my aunt, who worked for the welfare department in camp in Topaz [an internment camp in Utah], went and beat on her supervisor's door and managed to get them to send a wire saying they should send the remains back. And that way our family was able to verify the fact that he had died."[17]

Nakahata does not know the place of his father's death, a fact he called "really kind of sad if you think about it, that I don't know where he died."[18]

Eddie Sakamoto remembers when his father, who operated a fruit stand, was taken away from their Los Angeles-area home. On the evening of December 7, an FBI agent waited outside their home for the elder Sakamoto to return. His father was told "to get the suitcase and toothbrush and so forth," though Sakamoto says his father did not understand why he was being taken. Records show that he, too, was sent to Fort Missoula.[19]

Masuo Yasui was one of the many prominent businessmen detained at Fort Missoula. Yasui had come to the United States in 1903, settling first in Portland, Oregon, where he worked as a domestic, cook and gardener for five years before migrating to Hood River, Oregon. In Hood River he began a mercantile store with his brother and as the business prospered he bought farm and orchard lands in the area.[20] He reared thirteen children in the Methodist faith and put all thirteen through college.[21]

One of his sons, Minoru Yasui, an attorney who was commissioned a second lieutenant in the Army infantry reserve in 1937, was to become the first person to defy the orders that imposed curfews and travel restrictions on the Japanese. These American Japanese were ultimately ordered to leave the West Coast for detention in government-operated camps. Yasui's challenge would become one of the landmark cases decided by the Supreme Court pertaining to restrictions on the Japanese and their wholesale relocation from the West Coast.

By 1941 Masuo Yasui's business interests were worth an estimated half a million dollars.[22] His prominence in Hood River was not confined to the Japanese community. He was a member of the Rotary Club, a director of the Apple Growers Association, a pillar of the Hood River Methodist Church and a friend of many of the most prominent white residents of the town. He was arrested December 13, 1941, and his personal assets as well as the assets of the Yasui Brothers Company were frozen by the U.S. Treasury Department.[23] For the next several months he would live behind the barbed-wire confines of an abandoned Army fort.

Yasui, Sakamoto, Nakahata. These are but three of the twelve-hundred men who, against their will, with only the barest of necessities, were brought under a pall of suspicion to an alien place to await an uncertain future.

JAPANESE INTERNEES ARRIVE IN MISSOULA

T HE PRESENCE OF a thousand Italian seamen on the outskirts of
Missoula had sparked a curiosity among the townspeople that
diminished as the summer of 1941 faded to fall. But it was with more
than curiosity that Montanans greeted the Japanese in the last weeks of
December of 1941.

There were few Japanese among the state's 560,000 residents; the 1940
census counted just over 500 in Montana, many employed by the railroads.
Of the five hundred, 257 were identified by the Immigration and Naturalization Service in 1942 as Japanese-born aliens. [1]

When Japanese air and naval forces struck Pearl Harbor, the shock,
anger and frustration at an enemy thousands of miles away was turned
toward an enemy within reach. A man's looks were sufficient reason for
suspicion. The first reported incident in Montana following the Pearl Harbor attack came on the evening of December 7 when five Japanese railroad
workers were threatened with lynching. The five, B. Oato, 57, a Northern
Pacific Railroad foreman; W. Hamada, 67; T. Tetsuga, 67; K. Shinamura,
59, and A. Shinamura, 55, were held as a "measure of safety" in the jail
in Superior. All were later given rides to their homes in Livingston. [2]

A similar incident involving railway employees occurred the following day in Miles City. Employees at the Milwaukee Road shops refused
to work until seven Japanese co-workers were sent away. The Japanese
were escorted to their homes. [3]

Though there were no such incidents reported in Missoula, French
T. Ferguson, the editor of the *Missoulian* cautioned readers in a December
10 editorial against succumbing to hysterical acts:

"There is no excuse for anti-Japanese hysteria in this part of the United
States, far away from the scene of action, removed from any properties
or positions of great military importance. There should be no threats or
actual violence against harmless Japanese hereabouts.

"Hysteria should be avoided everywhere, for that matter. The Japanese
that are dangerous will be interned, promptly and safely. The ordinary
citizen does not need to worry about them.

"We are not going to win this war by losing our heads."

Ferguson continued to urge restraint in a similar editorial just two days
later. Noting that someone had chopped down four Japanese cherry trees
in Washington, D.C., he remarked:

"We're glad such a bit of hysterical vandalism didn't happen in Missoula.

"Such things will not win the war. Hard work and courage and sacrifice
and self-denial are the important things.

"Nobody can serve this nation in its time of greatest need by acting
as only a dim-wit should be expected to."

Facing page
**While the Italians at the
fort were recruited to
work in the community,
the Japanese that soon
were to arrive were kept
under tight guard.**
MONTANA HISTORICAL SOCIETY

This view of the fort complex in the early 1940s was taken by well-known Missoula photographer R.H. McKay. The 29 barracks buildings and the camp's auxiliary buildings are on the right. Remains of the CCC compound are along the river in the upper left. What is at present the Historical Museum at Fort Missoula complex is at the top. Many of the buildings shown are now gone. A portion of the Missoula Country Club golf course is in the lower left, along with the fort water tower. PICTORIAL HISTORIES COLLECTION

While no reports of anti-Japanese incidents in Missoula were published in either the *Missoulian* or the *Missoula Sentinel*, an allusion to the manner in which some townspeople were treating Missoula-area Japanese appeared just a week after Pearl Harbor. A Korean family that was interviewed pleaded with Missoulians to differentiate between Japanese and Koreans. "The C.S. Hahn family of Target Range reports that the now unsavory 'Jap' has been whispered hoarsely in stores and on the streets by local residents passing them," the paper said. The family pointed out that Koreans and Japanese are not of the same "stock." Harry Hahn, 20, "was quite vociferous in his condemnation of the Japanese and explained that his hatred could be traced back for centuries," the paper reported. Similar trouble was being reported by Koreans elsewhere. To avoid ugly incidents the Korean National Association of Los Angeles had instituted a "certified identification" system through which those who proved their nationality were issued cards and buttons identifying themselves, the paper noted.[4]

While the *Missoulian* was trying to minimize anti-Japanese hysteria, national news reports about the statements of federal officials were undermining such efforts. Roosevelt had sent Navy Secretary Frank Knox to Hawaii to investigate the attack on Pearl Harbor and how American naval forces had suffered such severe losses. Upon his return on December 15, while giving no details of fifth-column activity, he announced: "I think the most effective fifth-column work of the entire war was done in Hawaii, with the possible exception of Norway."[5] This allegation did not appear in any way, nor was it supported in any manner, in his subsequent report to Roosevelt, but its effect was to lay "major blame for the Pearl Harbor defeat at the door of the ethic Japanese in the United States."[6] In its investigation almost forty years later, the Commission on Wartime Relocation and Internment of Civilians stated: "Knox's statement was not only unfounded: it ignored the fact that Japanese Americans in large numbers had immediately come to the defense of the islands at the time of the attack."[7] The damage at home, where war news was censored, and statements such as these consequently carried great weight, was enormous, the commission concluded.

Nonetheless, Ferguson continued his crusade for caution, unmoved by Knox's inflammatory statements. Just a few days after his fifth-column comment, the paper said: "There were several Japanese-Americans who helped the U.S. Navy in the fight at Pearl Harbor. Remember these when you 'Remember Pearl Harbor.'"[8]

That type of cool-headed calm was not prevalent in the media, not even in the *Missoulian*'s national news columns. The media frequently aided in the propaganda flood that rushed from the federal government, and the Associated Press was often the channel through which it flowed. For example, in late December the Associated Press transmitted on its wires a photograph of an elderly Japanese man. The caption under the photograph read: "This ghost-like creature is Mitsuru Toysama, at 87 still a master in international intrigue. He heads the notorious Black Dragon Society, through which operates the Japanese fifth column that played such a big part in the treachery at Pearl Harbor."[9]

While the *Missoulian* wire editors succumbed to such propaganda, the newspaper's coverage locally was cautious and continually quoted people who urged restraint from readers in dealing with American Japanese. On the same day that the story of the Navy secretary's statements appeared on page one of the *Missoulian*, a story on page three contained a report of a speech to the local Lion's Club by the Rev. Gordon Bennett, in which the minister "opposed any hatred for the people not responsible for the war," namely the "Japanese and Germans in this country, many of whom are citizens and loyal to our government." Bennett asked Montanans to avoid "such absurdities as evidenced in the last war, such as throwing out German music and art or getting 'riled up' over simple things as changing German measles to Liberty measles."

But some Missoulians were not able to resist getting "riled up." Immigration Service supply officer Clyde Neu recalls an assignment in December 1941 in which, due to a shortage of border patrol guards, he was sent to Salt Lake City to pick up some Japanese who had been rounded up by the FBI and were to be interned at Fort Missoula. The train pulled into Butte on the return trip and a young Korean man, whose family had a truck garden in Butte, boarded for the trip to Missoula, where he planned to enlist at the area induction station. When the train arrived in Missoula with 25 Japanese, in addition to its other passengers, Neu saw that "they had every policeman in Missoula, they had the sheriff's office and all his deputies down there at the depot. You'd a thought we were going to come in there with this great big bunch of Japanese and be out of control and everything else."

When the Korean youth from Butte got off the train "three fellows had a hold of him down there (in the area for regular passengers) and were manhandling him," Neu recalls. He approached the men and asked, "What the hell are you doing with this fellow, anyway?"

"Well, he's trying to get away," the men answered.

"I said, 'He's trying to get in the Army!' I said, 'Hands off him.'"

"Well, he looked like a Japanese," Neu remembers they answered. [10]

The first public acknowledgment that Missoula would be home to Japanese aliens came when the Salt Lake City Japanese whom Neu was dispatched to accompany disembarked from the train on December 18. Observing the scene at the station, the *Missoulian* reported:

"The Japanese, most of them well-dressed and one slightly lame, carrying a cane got off the railroad car and walked quietly to the waiting bus. Their diminutive stature seemed to make them lose some dignity, perhaps even a little 'face' when they had to leave the car without benefit of a step." [11]

Interned Japs Arrive at Fort Missoula Camp

100 More Sons of Nippon, Italy and Germany Are Reported on Way Here.

After 25 interned Japanese aliens arrived at the Fort Missoula internment camp Thursday afternoon, officials of the camp indicated that more might arrive, but said they had no definite information.

(An Associated Press dispatch from San Francisco Thursday said a special train carrying approximately 100 German, Italian and Japanese aliens en route to Fort Missoula had left San Francisco Wednesday.

(The dispatch did not say when the aliens were scheduled to arrive in Missoula.)

From Salt Lake.

The 25 Japanese arriving here Thursday were rounded up in Salt Lake City, Utah, a Fort Missoula source said. They were placed in the southeast section of the camp, and were isolated from the thousand Italians who have been held at the camp for several months, this source said.

The entire eastern part of the camp is provided with new barracks which were constructed during the summer to raise the capacity to about 2,000 men.

About 75 or 100 persons were on hand when the Japanese arrived at 3 o'clock in the afternoon in an extra car attached to Northern Pacific train No. 1. The car was set

(Continued on Page 8, Column 5.)

The first Japanese arrived at Fort Missoula on Dec. 18, 1941. The *Missoula Sentinel* recorded their arrival.

In early 1942 the number of Japanese men detained at Fort Missoula reached more than 1,000. These new arrivals enter at the front gate.
MANSFIELD LIBRARY COLLECTION, UNIVERSITY OF MONTANA

A crowd had gathered at the station to bid goodbye to a number of soldiers who had recently enlisted, the *Missoulian* said, but it made no mention of the altercation that Neu recalls.

The newspaper said the contingent might be followed by additional prisoners because the Associated Press reported that a train had left San Francisco December 17 with 100 Germans, Italians and Japanese aboard, bound for Fort Missoula and Fort Lincoln, North Dakota.

Three-hundred-sixty-four "enemy alien" Japanese and 25 Italians arrived by rail on December 19 and were quickly spirited away to the fort. Nick Collaer, supervisor of alien detentions at Fort Missoula, said the Japanese were kept separate from the 900 Italians. He said the men, who were "quiet, orderly and very cooperative," were primarily West Coast businessmen whose wives and families remained at home. The Japanese, he said, expected harsh treatment at the fort but were "very much surprised at the kind treatment afforded them." Collaer told Missoulians to expect more Japanese in the days to follow.[12]

By the end of the year, 633 Japanese were detained at Fort Missoula. Federal agents continued arrests into 1942 and by April 1, 1942, the population at the fort was 2,003 men, roughly evenly divided between Japanese and Italians.[13] The average age of the Japanese men at the fort was 60 years.[14] There were no women detained. The prisoners' advanced years, coupled perhaps with the emotional hardship they endured in a detention camp far from family and familiar surroundings, took their toll. On the day the first group arrived by rail from California, one man died.

Records at the National Archives show that Seichiro Itou, of 308 East Third Street, Los Angeles, died at the fort on December 19. It is a spartan report; nothing is included about the age of the man, the details of his death, or the disposition of the body. He was the first of three Japanese to die at Fort Missoula. Shigekazu Hazanna, 843 Maple Avenue, Los Angeles, died March 1, 1942, and Kameki Kinoshita, Route 2, Tacoma, Washington, died April 1, 1942.

The daily routine for the interned Japanese was soon established. It was much the same as what had been worked out for the Italians, though the two groups had almost no interaction. Wide World news agency sent a reporter to the fort and this is the scene he described:

"It seems to be quite a problem out here to keep the hundreds of Italians and Japanese happy at the Fort Missoula concentration camp.

"They're living in a place that looks like an expensive summer resort. They get three squares a day. They have practically no work to do.

"But they still glower at each other. The camp guards never have seen an Italian say so much as 'good morning' to the Japanese. The internees just don't seem to grasp the kernel of the Axis philosophy—you know, that the Japanese and Italians have a lot in common and therefore should be happy as bugs-in-a-rug when they're together.

"So there had to be special arrangements at the Missoula camp.

"Of course, no one at all gets into the camp. The guards even arrest people who try to take pictures through the fence. But the stories circulate anyway through the pretty college town of Missoula.

The Japanese crafted vases from pebbles collected in the compound.
TIM GORDON COLLECTION

"The Japanese have picked on [sic] a curious pastime. They make gadgets from pebbles. Vases, bowls, what-nots. They'll sit alone for hours picking small pebbles from the gravel on the camp roads. Then they trot silently back to their quarters and stick them together into some sort of gadget. They all seem to have the fever. They work as intently as though they were digging a tunnel to Tokyo.

"The happy-go-lucky Italians vary. Some make ship models, very beautiful ones. Some get together and yodel opera arias. There are a few gifted painters. The rest just walk or 'set.'

"A few weeks ago the camp authorities felt they should recognize the prisoners' artistic urges. So they arranged a downtown exhibit of their work. Some of the pieces were sold.

"The camp is an old military fort. It's a handsome group of white buildings set at the edge of a really beautiful valley surrounded on all sides by really beautiful mountains. The air is sweet with clover. The days are warm and the nights cool enough for good sleeping.

"The Italians and Japanese are housed in separate buildings. It was . . . [a surprise to learn the Japanese and their] Axis brothers won't eat meals together.

"The men have to take care of themselves—clean their rooms, make their meals, do their own laundry. They rotate the duties.

"The authorities are splitting hairs to observe the Geneva convention on the treatment of war prisoners. That says, among other things, that prisoners should eat as well as soldiers.

"So the Missoula camp can spend each day for each prisoner the same amount of money spent to feed an American soldier.

Small barracks housed about 40 men each. The Japanese kept the grounds spotless.
HISTORICAL MUSEUM AT FORT MISSOULA COLLECTION

"They've decided to make the prisoners happy by giving them the food they're accustomed to. It takes quite a bit of housekeeping to split the orders: Spaghetti, olive oil and garlic for the Italians, and rice, soybeans and fish for the Japanese.

"There is a small cooking problem with the Italians. They're so casual about housekeeping that guards have to ramble through the kitchen periodically to point out spots that need a touch of soap.

"The Japanese are immaculate. Silent, you might almost say sullen — but immaculate.

"There's another little difficulty with the Italians. They all want what the next man has. The camp buys clothes for the prisoners. And when one Italian gets a new pair of shoes, there's a flood of requests from the other Italians for shoes. Not just shoes, but the exact tan oxford the first man got.

"This characteristic stirred up a little flurry when the Italians found out that some of their group, on special diets for diabetics, were getting special food. The camp suddenly had a big list of diabetics. Then the camp doctor noised it around that there are unpleasant phases to treating the disease, and pronto, the new diabetic cases made miraculous recoveries.

"The prisoners may see visitors any time. But they must either talk in English or in the presence of an interpreter. They can write and receive letters.

"Most of the day there's little to do. That's slightly irritating right now to Montana's sugar beet growers. They'd like to use some of the prisoners to harvest crops which may have to be sacrificed because of the shortage of labor here. But the rules say 'no.'

"There are no Germans in the camp. They're in another camp, with more Japanese. It seems the Japanese just snub both the Italians and the Germans, and receive snubs in return. But things happen when the Italians and Germans are housed together.

"The only group which hasn't caused trouble seems to be the Italian bakers, and they really like turning out good bread."[15]

Jerre Mangione, a government official who checked conditions at several of the Immigration Service detention camps, reported that the Japanese and Italians at the camp had little interaction, but that was by choice. He also reported a group of Germans were at the camp, though there are no detailed references to them in National Archives records.

"The longer I remained at Missoula the more aware I became of the lack of love between the Japanese, Germans, and Italians," he wrote. "The Japanese, who had their own mess hall, behaved as though the other two groups did not exist. The Germans and Italians, on the other hand, expressed open contempt for the Japanese, whom they regarded as inferior people, but they had a low opinion of one another. They were compelled to share the same mess hall, but since they could not agree on a common menu, they maintained separate cuisines, with the Italians turning up their noses at sauerkraut and the Germans disdaining spaghetti. Their general incompatibility sometimes resulted in fisticuffs, at which time their leaders would feel obliged to remind the men that they were allies, not enemies. All in all, the relationship between the three groups hardly augured well for the solidity of the Axis alliance. 'If, God forbid, the Axis powers should win the war,' an Italian seaman told me, 'there would soon be another war between the winners.'"[16]

Life for the Japanese at the fort was much as it had been for the Italians since May 1941. There were thirty-eight to forty people in each dormitory and every ten dormitories had their own mess hall, bathrooms and showers.[17]

In the spring of 1942 the Japanese began construction of a nine-hole

A group of Japanese from Hawaii organized their own softball team.
PICTORIAL HISTORIES COLLECTION

Missoula Mercantile.

golf course that one intern from Hawaii said "was almost as beautiful as that at Oahu Country Club, which did not admit Japanese as members but which they could see from certain parts of Nuuanu."[18] Other reports describe it as a miniature or a par 3 golf course, which is more likely, since the Japanese were not at the fort long enough to complete anything more ambitious.

Both the Italians and Japanese were able to get passes occasionally for visits to town, though always in those early months they were accompanied by guards. Kumaji Furuya recalls one shopping trip to the Missoula Mercantile, where he was astonished at the variety of goods available and curious about the stuffed animal heads that were mounted on the walls. He told author Patsy Sumie Saiki how the reception he received at the store made him ever grateful:

"Furuya bought some material and other items to be sent as gifts to his family in Honolulu. The salesgirl asked, 'Are you Mexican?'

"Here it comes, thought Furuya. 'No, I'm Japanese.'

" 'Japanese? Do you live in town?'

" 'No, we live in a camp a few miles from here. It's an internment center.'

" 'What's that?'

" 'That's where they keep some of the aliens of those countries against whom the U.S. is fighting this war. Countries like Germany, Italy, Japan . . .'

" 'Are you from Japan?'

" 'No, I'm from Hawaii.'

" 'But Hawaii is not our enemy, is it? Why do the Japanese from Hawaii have to be in an internment camp?'

" 'That's what we'd like to know,' Furuya smiled. His heart was full, as he inwardly blessed her. How wonderful it was, to be treated as just another human being, not an individual tainted with disloyalty."[19]

But nearly all Japanese were so tainted. At the war's outbreak Italian and German nationals were lumped with Japanese under restrictions that banned their possession of cameras, radios and firearms, required them to get photo identification, and restricted their movements to daylight hours no further than five miles from their homes. But it was only the Japanese who were ultimately forced to move en masse from their homes to guarded camps.

One outspoken early advocate of wholesale relocation of the Japanese was Texas Congressman Martin Dies, the chairman of the House Committee on Un-American Activities. In a thousand-page report released in early February 1942 he charged that the United States had been "lax, tolerant and soft toward the Japanese who have violated American hospitality."[20] He said both alien and American Japanese were spying for the Japanese government and that the focal point of fifth-column activity was on the West Coast. "The Japanese government's use of its fifth column in the Philippines and Hawaii is a sample of what the United States can expect from the Japanese fifth column located on our Pacific Coast when the time comes for the fifth column to strike," he said.[21]

Responding to the Dies report, the *Missoulian* again came to the defense of the Japanese. Ferguson said the paper agreed with Attorney General Francis Biddle that it would be "profoundly unwise and profoundly un-American" to intern the Japanese in America. Many of the Japanese are as loyal to the United States as is the most "ardent lover of freedom, ideals and institutions" and many have sons in the U.S. military, he noted. He speculated that many of them were living in the United States because they did not like their own government. "We must keep these people in this frame of mind," he cautioned. "Decent treatment during the time of war will do the trick."[22]

But national news reports, based on statements from both federal and local authorities in the towns from which the reports emanated, continued to paint a picture of the U.S. Japanese as the enemy. In a February 14 story about the arrest of 50 additional Japanese on the coast, the Associated Press said, in this instance without attribution, that the arrests "piled higher the stock of guns and radios seized" and included among those taken into custody six reserve officers in the imperial Japanese army. On March 4 an AP story out of Los Angeles began: "Southern Californians, who long have known that Japanese had infiltrated into vital defense areas, had that fact emphasized today in startling clarity." The story was about the Los Angeles district attorney's press conference at which he exhibited a map illustrating land leases held by the Japanese "in or adjoining nearly every strategic region hereabouts."[23]

Those strategic locations included farmland near airports, railroads, dams, industrial parks and adjacent to power lines. But, according to author Michi Weglyn, there was a reason for that. The land was cheap because it was considered undesirable. In her book, *Years of Infamy*, Weglyn comments:

"It was a common practice among the Issei to snatch up strips of marginal unwanted land which were cheap: swamplands, barren desert areas that Caucasians disdained to invest their labor in. Often it included land bordering dangerously close to high-tension wires, dams, and railroad tracks. The extraordinary drive and morale of these hard-working frugal Issei who could turn parched wastelands, even marshes, into lush growing fields—usually with help from the entire family—became legendary."[24]

Though not nearly as intense as they were in California, the sentiments of some people in the Missoula area had an anti-Japanese taint. In mid-February the first letters addressing the Japanese "problem" began to appear in the *Missoulian*. Archie R. Randles noted that there had been some discussion of moving aliens from the West Coast to the Rocky Mountain region to alleviate the farm labor shortage. "Unless we are on guard these 'evacuees' may turn out to be Japs," he warned. "To relieve any 'shortage' we can welcome white evacuees, but no Japs, please." Randles said he didn't mean to doubt the loyalty of all Japanese Americans, but "it is the risk of luring the questionable ones into our market" that had to be avoided. Those questionable ones, he warned, "could act as firebugs" in the national forests. He ended his letter: "No Japs, please. No Japs, please. No Japs, please."[25]

It wasn't only sabotage of the forests that alarmed some western Montanans. Mrs. Walter Luke wrote in a letter published February 27, 1942, that proposals to bring aliens to Montana to help build highways might prove costly. "Had there been less desire to procure cheap labor there wouldn't be so many of these aliens in our country now," she said. She opposed bringing Japanese into Montana for any purpose and scoffed at the idea that moving them inland, away from vital coastal industries, would be an acceptable solution.

Many Montana businesses are vital to the war effort, she said, and "are not beyond being blown sky high." She said the forests and grain fields "could easily be reduced to ashes and our wild game eliminated completely; so there would be little need for roads if those treacherous Japs came here and started their sabotage."

Her solution was to "work to get the industries in here and keep the Japs out."[26]

The following day a man who signed his missive "Joe Kalispell" said he also opposed the use of alien labor in the state because of the danger to forests. He proposed that detention camps be built inland in California. "Some of the good people out there have been happy to have them around as long as they could profit by their cheap labor; when the tide turns they are anxious to palm them off on someone else," he wrote.

Some Montanans were also anxious to rid themselves of any aliens. In the same issue as the "Joe Kalispell" letter, the *Missoulian* published a brief story about Whitefish railroad union members who had passed a resolution asking that enemy aliens be fired from Great Northern Railway jobs. They also began circulating a petition to prevent Japanese from holding any jobs in the area in any capacity.

Worries about sabotage of the forests were not just a concern of some in western Montana. The state's eastern district congressman, Democrat

James F. O'Connor, said in late February 1942 that "thousands of Japs are being taken off the West Coast—but we don't want them." He warned that a match could burn up all the forests, fields and grain in the state. "Those Japs should be put in concentration camps and kept there," he said in a story from Washington, D.C., that was carried on the national news wires.[27]

The *Missoulian* acknowledged its readers' fears in a February 28 editorial, noting that while such apprehension was probably ungrounded, public opinion had to be considered in any plan to import Japanese labor:

"The West Coast is anxious to get rid of its Japanese. Taking the fifth column activities of Hawaiian Japs as an example, the Native Sons and others on the western shore expect the worst at home. And, perhaps they are right in this expectation, although it is likely that many American-born Japanese are loyal to this country.

"At the same time nobody wants the Western Japs, even in detention camps. Several hundred of them are confined at Fort Missoula now and appear to be a harmless lot, but Montana people do not like the idea of letting them work on the farms and in the woods of this district on account of fear of sabotage. To be sure, this attitude may do injustice to the hundreds of the transplanted Orientals but it exists and must be considered.

"It is regretted, in a way, because there is prospect of a lack of labor in at least some of the Western districts and interned Japanese undoubtedly could be used to advantage—including theirs. But unless the public mood should change, there is a definite prospect that this will not be done."

Though Montanans were uncomfortable with the prospect of Japanese moving inland, on the West Coast pressure to remove all Japanese was mounting. Fear that a full-scale invasion of the United States mainland was imminent grew stronger as the Japanese victories continued in the Pacific.

On March 2, Lt. Gen. John DeWitt, commanding general of the Western Defense Command, announced that all aliens would be removed from the West Coast, beginning first with the Japanese. "Germans and Italians will be evacuated later," he said. They never were.[28]

Once the evacuations were ordered, the *Missoulian* began a retreat from its previous position of condemning anti-Japanese action. Loyal American Japanese now had the opportunity to prove the degree of their patriotism, the paper said, explaining that because it was impossible to differentiate between the loyal and disloyal, all Japanese had to be evacuated. "This will not be too great a sacrifice for those who want to see Allied victory," Ferguson wrote.[29]

On April 1 the Associated Press relayed a story from Los Angeles saying that 500 Japanese had arrived at an assembly center near there and "without exception the evacuees seemed philosophically happy."[30] When the removal was completed in early June, an Associated Press dispatch from San Francisco began: "A mass movement without precedent in American history, the evacuation of the West Coast's entire Japanese population of almost 100,000 was ended today.

"It proceeded without any great hardship, and almost without incident."[31] But before the evacuation was over, nearly 120,000 Japanese, the majority of them American citizens, were removed from their homes and sent first to relocation or assembly centers and then to detention camps. Most had only a few weeks' notice. They were to bring only what could be carried in small suitcases. Homes, possessions, crops, businesses — all were left untended or sold by he Japanese before leaving for only pennies on the dollar. These 120,000 people of Japanese extraction now joined the ranks of the thousand Japanese held since early 1942 at Fort Missoula, detained by their own government solely because they shared a common ancestry.

LOYALTY HEARINGS AT FORT MISSOULA

W HAT SHOULD BE DONE about the Japanese? The answer to that question on the American mainland was no simpler than it was in the Pacific war theater, where Allied forces were being beaten badly in the first six months of the war. At home the "dangerous" Japanese were behind barbed wire in Montana and North Dakota. Did the Constitution allow them to be held indefinitely without charge or without trial? What about those Japanese who were not detained? Where did their loyalties lie? For both the Japanese already interned and those still at large, though living under rigid restrictions, the government's answer was to hold hearings. Missoulians were to play key roles in those hearings both for interned Japanese and those still living on the West Coast.

Democrat John Tolan was a California congressman selected to head a committee that would conduct hearings ostensibly to determine the fate of the West Coast Japanese. The House Select Committee Investigating National Defense Migration, dubbed the Tolan Committee, was authorized by Congress to investigate the proposal for exclusion of the Japanese from the West Coast. However, the hearings began after President Roosevelt signed Executive Order 9066 that permitted the military to order the evacuation of any persons from designated military zones. Because the executive order allowed the military to order evacuations, but gave it no power to enforce penalties for the failure to evacuate, it fell to Congress to authorize those sanctions. The Tolan committee, then, held its hearings with the understanding that the evacuations of the Japanese were certain. Its job became one of whether to support or oppose the executive order by persuading Congress to either reject or impose penalties for the failure to obey the exclusion orders. Upon its return to Washington in March the committee "was eager to see that the property of aliens was safeguarded by the government and wanted the Army to be concerned about hardship cases in an evacuation," but was "unwilling to challenge the need for Executive Order 9066 and the evacuation," a later review of its actions concluded.[1]

Tolan's name was thus to become solidly linked with the mass evacuation. But his name was familiar to many Missoulians before his committee hearings brought him national notice. Born in 1877 in Minnesota, he received his law degree from the University of Kansas in 1902. His first job out of law school was as county attorney of Deer Lodge County, Montana, a post he held from 1902 to 1906. He then practiced law in Missoula, until moving to Oakland, California, in 1915. He was first elected to Congress in 1935.

Tolan's hearings were widely publicized and agitators for the removal of the Japanese used them to further inflame public opinion. One of the strongest advocates for relocation and internment of all Japanese was California Attorney General Earl Warren, later the chief justice of a United States Supreme Court noted primarily for its attention to ensuring and expanding all Americans' civil liberties. It was a statement made by Earl Warren to the Tolan committee that is credited as "the single most powerful voice for the ultimate decision of the United States government to remove all persons of Japanese ancestry from the Western Defense Command,"[2] a military designation for the coastal areas of California, Oregon and Washington. Warren told Tolan's committee:

"I am afraid many of our people in other parts of the country are of the opinion that because we have had no sabotage and no fifth column activities in this state since the beginning of the war, that means that none have been planned for us. But I take the view that this is the most ominous sign in our whole situation.

"It convinces me more than perhaps any other factor that the sabotage that we are to get, the fifth column activities that we are to get, are timed just like Pearl Harbor was timed. . . .

"I want to say that the consensus of opinion among law enforcement officers in this state is that there is more potential danger among the group of Japanese who were born in this country than from the alien Japanese who were born in Japan."[3]

Warren said there was no way to sort the loyal from the disloyal. He asserted: ". . . when we are dealing with the Caucasian race we have methods that will test the loyalty of them. . . . But when we deal with the Japanese we are in an entirely different field and we cannot form any opinion that we believe to be sound."[4]

Warren was not alone in expressing this idea that because the Japanese had not yet been disloyal only proved they could not be trusted. While the Hearst newspapers had long ago taken up the cause of defaming the Japanese, this anti-Asian sentiment was by mid-February being sounded by even respected journalists. In his syndicated column of February 14, 1942, Walter Lippmann charged that the fact no sabotage had been undertaken was a "sign that the blow is well-organized and that it is held back until it can be struck with maximum effect." Three days later journalist Westbrook Pegler echoed Lippmann's contention and said the Japanese should be moved from the coast and held under armed guard and "to hell with habeas corpus."[5]

The hearings for the Japanese at Fort Missoula were conducted by Alien Enemy Hearings Boards, comprising citizens selected by the Justice Department who served without pay. Ironically, one member of the Montana board was Mike Mansfield, an instructor in history and political science at the University of Montana. Mansfield was to win a seat in Congress in the fall of 1942, beginning a political career that would be marked by record tenure as majority leader of the U.S. Senate and as the United States ambassador to Japan.

Hearing boards from various locations in the Northwest convened at Fort Missoula in early February. The boards would interrogate those Japanese from board members' cities or states, but when their caseloads were especially heavy, the Montana board would assist them. Their task was to question each of the men individually to determine which were dangerous enemy aliens." Transcripts of the hearings would be forwarded to the United States attorney general for review, but no announcements would be made in Missoula as to the outcome of the investigations.[6]

Members of the Montana hearing board, in addition to Mansfield, were Charles W. Leaphart, the chairman, who was dean of the University of Montana School of Law; E.C. Mulroney, vice-chairman, a Missoula attorney; and John Slattery, a Great Falls lawyer.[7]

Other boards from Los Angeles, San Francisco, Seattle, Spokane, Oregon, Utah and Nevada also held hearings in Missoula beginning in late January and ending in late June.

The Oregon board's members were William G. Everson, president of Linfield College, McMinnville, Oregon; Colonel Alfred E. Clark, a Portland attorney; Leslie N. Scott, the state treasurer from Salem; Carl C. Donaugh, Portland, the United States attorney for Oregon, and Allen F. Davis, a special agent of the Federal Bureau of Investigation.

In early February the Oregon board heard the case of Masuo Yasui, the Hood River businessman. His son, Minoru Yasui, who was to defy the curfew orders in late March, received permission to travel to Missoula to assist in his father's defense.

Mike Mansfield, 1942.
UNIVERSITY OF MONTANA LIBRARY

"With headlines screaming about the furious battles for Bataan, it was intimidating to realize that, being physically Japanese, there was no assurance of being able to get a hotel room or even being able to go to a restaurant in Missoula," he recalled. "In short, I was scared and alone in hostile territory. After arriving I was able to get a hotel room, and I hired a taxi to go out to Fort Missoula, to the internment center. There, surrounded by barbed wire, guarded by armed MPs, I went into the office to try to arrange to see the various internees from Oregon."[8]

Yasui was allowed to visit his father and to attend his hearing before the board, but was not permitted to talk with any other Japanese.

"The hearings were a complete farce," he wrote. "The official for the Enemy Control Unit pointed out that my father was an influential leader in the Japanese community in Hood River, Oregon; that he had extensive property interests; that he had visited Japan for a summer vacation for three months in 1925; that he had been awarded a medal by the Emperor of Japan for promoting U.S.-Japan relations; and that he had been instrumental in obtaining a position with the consulate general of Japan in Chicago for me.

"The most incredible thing was when they produced childlike drawings of the Panama Canal showing detailed drawings of how the locks worked. The hearing officer took these out and asked, 'Mr. Yasui, what are these?' Dad looked at the drawings and diagrams and said, 'They look like drawings of the Panama Canal.' They were so labeled, with names of children. Then the officer asked my father to explain why they were in our home. 'If they were in my home,' my father replied, 'it seems to me that they were drawings done by my children for their schoolwork.' The officer then asked, 'Didn't you have these maps and diagrams so you could direct the blowing up of the canal locks?' My father said, 'Oh, no! These are just schoolwork of my children.' The officer said, 'No, we think you've cleverly disguised your nefarious intent and are using your children merely as a cover. We believe you had intent to damage the Panama Canal.' To which my father vehemently replied, 'No, no, no!' And then the officer said pointedly, 'Prove that you didn't intend to blow up the Panama Canal!' I can still remember so vividly the officer asking my father to prove that he didn't intend to blow up the Panama Canal!

"Why a businessman and agriculturist with an impeccable reputation, living in a far-off rural town like Hood River—two hundred miles from the ocean, and possibly three thousand miles from the Panama Canal—should have to prove that he had no intent to blow up the Panama Canal seemed to me then, and seems to me now, to be the height of absurdity.

"It was on this kind of 'evidence' that my father and thousands of others were confined to internment camps, operated by the U.S. Department of Justice and manned by the U.S. Army, and were kept for the duration, until the spring of 1946."[9]

Quaker missionary Herbert Nicholson was associate pastor of the West Los Angeles Japanese church, the only Caucasian ministering to an all-Japanese church. Because he knew so many of the Los Angeles-area Japanese interned at Fort Missoula, he came to Missoula in March to see whether he could assist any of the men during their hearings. The Justice Department allowed him to serve as an interpreter for some of the men from California and Nevada. The Nevada board's members were "Dr. Johnson, who had been a Baptist minister and now [was] a professor of philosophy at the University of Nevada; a man named Smith who was head of the Falcon newspaper in Carson City, and another man who was a lawyer."[10]

Nicholson said the hearings began with a Federal Bureau of Investigation agent acting as prosecutor, asking the Japanese, "Why are you here?" Each answered, "I don't know. I don't know." "Well, you are here because we suspect you of being a dangerous character," Nicholson remembers the agent responding. "That is all, they didn't give any reason."[11]

Half of the 52 hearings in which he acted as an interpreter were for Japanese men who worked at a copper mine in Nevada. Nicholson said: "But do you know what was the matter with the fifty men? Once a month this foreman would take fifty cents out of their pay and send it to Japan to help with the orphans and widows of men who had died in the war. They had a society that collected money to help orphans and widows of soldiers who had died in Japanese wars. Some of them didn't even know that the money was taken out. They had all come over as young fellows before they could be taken in the Japanese army. There was sort of an obligation to pay this fifty cents because they hadn't served in the army."[12]

Nicholson said the board members asked inane questions that made his anger rise.

"They always asked the same question. The professor of philosophy would always ask, 'What's your philosophy of life?' Asking these poor laborers their philosophy of life! I told them, 'Don't ask that question.'

"The whole thing was a farce, an absolute joke. I didn't see how these reasonable, intelligent university graduates and professors with Ph.d's could carry on a thing like that. I just couldn't understand. It was absurd."[13]

The Japanese miners were not unhappy to be at Fort Missoula, Nicholson said, because they told him working conditions in the mines were so bad they preferred internment.

Nicholson was not paid for his work, his transportation costs or his room and board while in Missoula. Nothing was offered by the government, but had it been he said he "wouldn't take anything from the government for this work. It's a lot of foolishness." One woman whose husband Nicholson tried to help asked him when he returned to Los Angeles what his train trip had cost. When he told her it was fifty dollars, she tried to reimburse him, but he refused the money. [14]

One aspect of the Missoula camp comforted the Quaker minister. His praise for Nick Collaer was effusive. Collaer held most of the Japanese at the fort in high regard. Judging from the letters they wrote their children and those they received in return, "these are the most loyal people we have in America," Nicholson said Collaer told him. The director said he believed their internment was "all caused by the pressure of public opinion" whipped up by people on the coast who didn't wish to compete with the Japanese in business and by the "Sons of the Golden West, these extremely anti-Japanese folks."

When the Montana hearing board met in mid-February, the *Missoulian* published a story about its task that lent an aura of high drama to the proceedings. "In a courtroom cloaked with secrecy, there is enacted each day at the Fort Missoula detention enter a small drama which is richly deserving of the notation because of its role in wartime," the story began. [15] The paper said the drama centered on "little publicized trials" for the detainees. The Montana board's task was to help the California boards, since so many of the Japanese at the fort were from that state. Before the Californians arrived, the Montana board had been busy "analyzing the data presented to make the required recommendations." The paper termed it a "wearying task as each alien case takes an average of an hour and a half, and sometimes the appeals take an entire morning or afternoon."

The *Missoulian* described the actual hearings this way:

"Each of the 500-odd Japanese detainees is interviewed if he wishes and each is allowed a fair trial. Civilians are barred from the court and nobody except the judges knows what judgment is passed upon each alien case. The courtroom trials are witnessed by only the judge presiding, witnesses or friends of the Japanese appearing, an FBI agent, an assistant district attorney and an interpreter. As each Japanese is interviewed (about six or eight constitute a day's work), he is questioned and cross examined by the judge after hearing testimony presented by the Federal Bureau of

Investigation, evidence by the assistant United States attorney, and, finally, more evidence by friends of the 'case.' "[16]

The board could make one of three decisions:
· Internment for the duration of the war.
· Release on parole to return home.
· Unconditional release, which would place the detained man in the "custody" of an American citizen.

When the Seattle hearing board returned to Washington after a stint at Fort Missoula, Gerald D. Hile, an assistant United States attorney, gave an interview to the *Seattle Times* in which he reported his impressions of the Fort Missoula camp, its prisoners and their treatment. He said the Japanese were as well-fed as American soldiers, though the cost to feed each man at Fort Missoula was 30 cents a day, compared with 48 cents for a United States soldier. The government, he said, was following the Geneva Convention requirements strictly in the hope that United States soldiers held by Japan would get reciprocal treatment.

"And it is cheaper to keep them happy," the *Missoulian* quoted the *Times* as reporting. "If they were mistreated, the number of guards would have to be increased."

Most of the men, Hile said, wanted to be with their families, but were otherwise not unhappy. Many who normally worked thirteen hours a day "consider their internment a vacation," he said.

He reported that their movements inside the camp were unrestricted and that some had plans for flower and vegetable gardens in the spring. None, he said, had attempted escape or suicide. As for their allegiance, Hile said: "While most of the Japs contend they are loyal to the United States, a few of them are not hesitant to let it be known that they hope Japan wins the war."[17]

Members of the Seattle board, in addition to Hile, were Seattle attorneys J. Speed Smith and Frank E. Holman, and Orting banker Leslie A. Stone.

In late February the Justice Department had concluded hearings for 1,084 enemy aliens. Based on the findings, the department held 448 for indefinite detention, released 215 and paroled 421. These were not just Missoula cases; by the end of February there were 193 hearing boards deciding the cases of more than five thousand aliens.[18]

Hearings for the Japanese in Missoula were not concluded until the last California board finished its business at the end of June. Members of that board were Stephen A. Farrand, Los Angeles, the chairman; Clayton Howland, Harry Wishard, David R. Rubin, a Los Angeles attorney, and Gardner Turrill, a Los Angeles banker. John Slattery, the Great Falls attorney who sat on the Montana board, assisted the California board.[19]

Slattery later told a Great Falls service club about the "spies" the board discovered during the hearing. The *Great Falls Tribune* reported his speech:

"He mentioned several individual cases of high ranking Japanese who he said probably would have been valuable in the councils of the military group in power in their own country but evidently were believed to be of greater use to it doing spy work over here.

"Most alien Japs, Slattery said, when asked whether they wanted this country or their own to win the war would try to avoid the question, but

when pressed would say that for their children over here they wished to see Uncle Sam victorious, but deep down in their hearts they were for their own country.

"Slattery said he enjoyed the reputation of being the 'tough man' on the enemy alien hearing board and was glad to say that he was to a considerable extent responsible for a lot of dangerous Japanese aliens being sent to places where they can do no more harm to this nation."[20]

The Department of Justice was not the only government agency scrutinizing the Japanese at Fort Missoula. Government agent Lewis Penwell interrogated each of the men, but it wasn't their loyalty that interested him. Penwell was an Internal Revenue Service agent from Helena, assigned to make sure each of the interned men paid taxes. Penwell reported that the 950 Japanese had a variety of vocations, including fisherman, merchant, poultry ranch operator, minister and accountant. One man raised canaries and another operated a fishery business that extended from the "Gulf of Mexico to the Pacific," he said. Their incomes ranged from nothing to a thousand dollars a month. Penwell said the men would not be charged a penalty if their income taxes were not paid by March 15 [the former deadline for paying federal income tax], as long as they filed an affidavit showing they were interned. Internal Revenue Service regulations applied to these Japanese the same as to any Americans, he said, except that those who had relatives, such as wives or children, living in Japan could not claim them as dependents. The Italians at the fort were not asked to pay taxes as none had any income.[21]

While awaiting the outcome of loyalty hearings conducted by civilian hearing boards, the detainees spent their time fashioning craft items.
MONTANA HISTORICAL SOCIETY COLLECTION

Penwell reported later, in a story the *Missoulian* headlined "Japs Required to Pay Shares of War's Cost," that income taxes owed by the Fort Missoula Japanese ranged from one dollar to twelve thousand dollars. He said the taxes of several were difficult to calculate because many had investments and had been away from their businesses for several months and were without the necessary information. "One who is a breeder and dealer in canary birds wanted to turn a bird in as a tax payment," the paper noted.[22]

Though the Missoula community accepted a thousand "dangerous" Japanese at Fort Missoula with barely a ripple of public resentment, a humanitarian gesture by the new president of Montana State University [now the University of Montana] in the spring of 1942 evoked angry protest.

The president of the University of Washington wrote MSU President Ernest O. Melby, inquiring whether the Missoula school would accept Japanese students ordered to leave the Seattle campus when all Japanese were evacuated from the Western Defense Command. Melby said he could "see no reason" why MSU could not take a "limited number of students," but cautioned that he would have to consult with the school's budget and policy committee and the Board of Education.[23]

As soon as Melby's sentiments were made public, opponents organized a lobbying effort to thwart the transfer of any Japanese students to MSU. Leading the opposition was Missoula lawyer Howard Toole, who attempted to shortstop the Melby plan by lining up the governor against it. He wrote to Governor Sam Ford:

"Dear Governor: I called you by phone yesterday because I was anxious to stop any possible reaction which might occur in this community from Dr. Melby's suggestion that Japanese students might be acceptable at the University. This community, as you know, has just gone through considerable discussion, with substantial opposition, to bringing in Japanese labor. . . .

"Dr. Melby's statement came out in the morning *Missoulian*, on the same day when the Missoula County draft numbers were announced. . . . One woman, whose son has a low draft number and is a junior at the University thought that her son would be called immediately, before he could finish this academic year. She was quite hysterical about the prospect that a Japanese might be permitted to come here to more-or-less take his place. Numerous other people have spoken to me about the matter, and they all seem to feel about the same way.

". . . I am also sure that many people in Montana will be reluctant to send their children to college where Japanese students are invited or accepted. It is pretty generally felt that the American-educated Japanese have been largely responsible for the strategical advantage the Japs have had over us in this war."

Toole added a hand-written postscript: "In fact, there is just plain hell to pay in this town about Dr. Melby's statement."[24]

His was not the only penned protest Ford received. The Missoula Chapter of the Disabled American Veterans wrote Ford of its members' concern for the safety of any Japanese sent to the Missoula school. A Montana American Legion resolution forwarded to the governor was more explicit. Japanese students' safety could not be guaranteed, the Legion said, either at the hands of "American students" or those parents who lost sons "at the treacherous hand of Nippon."[25]

The Anaconda Commercial Club also expressed its unhappiness over Melby's plan, telling Governor Ford that it would be unfair to admit such students to any institution "supported entirely by the taxpayers of the State of Montana and not by any Japanese interest."[26]

On April 14 the Board of Education met in closed session for three hours to discuss whether to admit any Japanese to MSU. It decided to make no decision "because of the lateness of the school year."[27] Deferring a decision kept the Japanese out of the university for the 1942 school year. Melby did not let the matter die, however. In July he suggested that the question should be left to the school administration. It was his intention to allow some to attend. "The University at Missoula may, if given the opportunity, admit a few carefully selected Japanese students," he told the Board of Education.[28]

Ernest O. Melby
UNIVERSITY OF MONTANA
LIBRARY

Twelve prospective students had already asked to be admitted, including seven from Washington, three from California and two from Oregon. Half were women and most had previously attended other colleges. A thirteenth student, a woman who had transferred to MSU from the University of Washington before the Board of Education took up the issue, attended the Montana school during spring quarter. She was allowed to stay, but the twelve others were refused entry.[29]

Both sides of the debate were aired in the *Missoulian* letters column. Jim Boyack called the board's decision "undemocratic and unpatriotic."

"I submit that there can be no more positive way of insuring the continuance of our way of life than to be educating those honest, sincere Japanese-American citizens of the United States in our own school and in our own ideals. Refusal to do so forces those who would be our best citizens and friends into the position of having to be our enemies. Such an act surely must be classed as unpatriotic.

"Furthermore, to refuse those who desire to become good citizens the right to do so is a direct announcement to all that it is not justice for which we are fighting. It is an announcement that we will fight from a prejudice that is as blind and unintelligent as that of which we accuse our enemies."[30]

Archie Randles, one of the paper's frequent letter-writers, argued that

Gov. Sam C. Ford
DeWALT STUDIO PHOTO
MONTANA HISTORICAL
SOCIETY ARCHIVES

allowing Japanese to attend MSU would be dangerous and unwise. The premier of Japan was educated in the United States, he said, and was "the most American-hating Jap of all Nippon." While he conceded that some Japanese Americans were undoubtedly loyal, he said surely they could " 'excuse please' our raised eyebrows under the circumstances." He said admitting them to the Montana university that is so close to interned Japanese at Fort Missoula "would work a hardship on the Jap students and the officials, Federal and civil and college." He asked whether there could be any guarantee that American-educated Japanese would not go back to Japan after the war "and prepare for another Pearl Harbor."[31]

Though the *Missoulian* never commented editorially on the debate over whether to admit Japanese students to Montana State University, its policy of tolerance for Japanese Americans was reversed in late March and the paper began to attack the Japanese editorially. It said "thoughtful" Americans had suspected since December 7 that Japanese in Hawaii had aided the attack on Pearl Harbor and stated as fact that Japanese fishermen from the island greeted the invaders in naval uniforms. Quoting "veteran Far East correspondent" Mark J. Gayn, the paper said: " 'The Japs,' he says, 'have the most vicious and long-ranged fifth column activities that the war has yet seen.' 'They might win the war,' he warns, 'if we allow overconfidence to make us slow and unwilling to make sacrifices or take risks.' "

The paper added its own views: "Or, we might add, to take precautions against Japanese espionage or sabotage. We are glad to see that this danger at least is appreciated fully and that Western Japanese are being put where they can do no harm. We have learned at least the first part of the Jap lesson."[32]

The once-benevolent attitude displayed toward American Japanese was gone. It was a harsh about-face. While those bitter words had no effect on the Fort Missoula Japanese, they reflected an attitude of hate that at Fort Missoula would soon turn into action.

"YOU LYING YELLOW SON-OF-A-BITCH!"

W HILE ALIEN HEARING BOARDS were investigating the loyalties of the hapless Japanese, Immigration Service immigrant inspectors were busy interrogating many Japanese at Fort Missoula who they suspected were in the United States illegally. Those interrogations created an incident with international repercussions considered so potentially severe that the United States government kept information about it under wraps for more than forty years.

The incident began when Herman Schwandt, an inspector in charge of detention and deportation, came to Fort Missoula from Seattle in late March 1942, bringing with him some Japanese who were to be detained in the compound. While in an office building at the fort, he overheard these shouted remarks: "You lying yellow son-of-a-bitch, you have been lying long enough! If you don't tell the truth now I am going to knock your teeth down your throat!"[1]

Schwandt reported what he had overhead and the Justice Department immediately launched an investigation. What caused apprehension in Washington, however, was a formal complaint filed with the State Department in June 1942 through the Spanish consulate in San Francisco. The International Red Cross had been told of claims of mistreatment when a representative visited Fort Missoula. It was reported to the Spanish ambassador, whose embassy acted on Italy's behalf since diplomatic relations between the United States and Italy were severed when war was declared. The United States government was particularly concerned that any mistreatment be stopped because it feared reprisals against Americans held in enemy countries if word of mistreatment spread.[2]

The Justice Department's investigation into the matter was swift and thorough but kept a closely guarded secret. Only in December 1985 did the government declassify the records and open the files to the public.

What happened in Missoula? Many of the Japanese detained at the fort were trying to prove they had come to the United States to live permanently previous to 1924 because that was the year Congress shut off Japanese immigration. Any Japanese not already in the United States by July 1, 1924, could be deported. Some of the Japanese lied during the interrogations to protect themselves from deportation. A few Japanese lied to protect friends in the country illegally.[3]

Karl I. Zimmerman, chief supervisor of immigration for the Immigration and Naturalization Service, was assigned to investigate allegations of mistreatment. In his report of June 29, 1942, he outlined the charges:

Yazaemon Abe claimed that while waiting to be questioned he was slapped by Immigrant Inspector Martin H. Herstrom Jr. Once inside the interrogation room, Senior Patrol Officer Harold W. Brown pulled his hair, hit him on the neck with his fist and slapped his head. Interpreter Chai

Hoon Kim "pushed him in the stomach four or five times." Abe claimed that the abuse he received caused him to bleed from the mouth. After his appearance before the inspectors he was placed in solitary confinement in the guardhouse for three days. The solitary confinement cell had no toilet facilities and was barely large enough for one person. He also said he was forced to sign a statement that was not true.

Hachiro Ozaki said while he was being questioned on March 14, 1942, Herstrom "made a motion as though he were going to kick" him, threw burned match sticks and wads of paper at his face, tried to get him to say untruthfully that he had entered the United States illegally from Mexico after 1924 and then confined him to the guardhouse for several days. Later, during another interrogation session, he claimed he was slapped several times by interpreter Edward Pai. He said on other occasions his face was slapped "so often that it was impossible for him to count the number of times," his toes were stepped on, his chest was poked and Herstrom struck his throat.

Japanese doctor Kozo Tamaki told Ernest J. Hover, supervisor of special investigations for the Immigration Service, that he treated Ozaki for an injury to his shin that Dr. Tamaki judged was caused by a forceful blow of a foot.

Tomekichi Kubota told Dr. Tamaki that an immigration officer "rammed his elbow" into Kubota's ribs "with a shoulder movement."

Rinzo Saito claimed Herstrom grabbed him and shook him and he was several times made to stand for entire days and denied lunch.

Tsunenosuke Owada, who was characterized in Zimmerman's report as "very confused," claimed he was struck, slapped, pushed, hit lightly with an empty bottle, had his mouth forced open when someone jammed fingers into it, was verbally abused, deprived of lunch and confined to the guardhouse for long periods. Camp records show he was jailed from March 19 through April 15. Ayao Matsushima, another Japanese detained at the fort, testified that Owada told him about all this and said it occurred in the room near where other camp personnel worked, but after regular working hours.

Hidenori Arima claimed he was called a liar, pushed down a hall and struck by Inspector Harold Brown and threatened with confinement in jail if he did not sign a statement that Arima claimed was untrue. He was jailed from March 17 through April 7.

Dr. Ajika Amano, a Japanese physician living in the same barracks as Arima, told Hover that he saw Arima return from one hearing with a "badly swollen" face. Dr. Amano said he "heard that the Korean interpreters were very cruel" and "handled the Japanese pretty bad." One of the immigration officers would often "press neck" of the Japanese, he said. Another Japanese internee, Soshicki Uno, said he also saw Armia's black eye.[4]

Yanezo Miyagishima said in the Zimmerman report that Inspector Herstrom kicked a chair out from under him and he was slapped so hard it affected his hearing temporarily. He complained about being confined to the guardhouse and the camp hospital, though he later admitted much of his confinement was at his request because he was being harassed by other Japanese in the compound. Records show he was in the guardhouse from February 20 through February 26, and from March 3 through March 6. On March 7 he was confined in the camp hospital, where he stayed until May 25.

Miyagishima did have problems with other detainees. His testimony during his first appearance before the immigration inspectors as to his immigrant status was at odds with what others had testified about him. Consequently, those Japanese who tried to make a case for Miyagishima's legal-alien status by swearing that he had been in the United States without interruption since before 1924 were threatened with perjury charges.

During his initial hearing on February 20, Miyagishima said he first came to the United States in March 1935, arriving on the ship Chichibu Maru in San Francisco. He said he posted a $500 bond that permitted him to enter the country for six months as a visitor. He admitted he had a wife and two teen-age children living in Japan and said his brother, Umeo Miyagishima, who was also detained at Fort Missoula, likewise had a wife and young children who had never been to the United States. He said Umeo had left Japan in 1938, making his third trip to the United States. All these statements were cause for the Immigration Service to deport both Yonezo and Umeo Miyagishima and were contrary to the testimony of several other Japanese, who said they had seen the brothers in the United States every day since the early 1920s.

When word of Yonezo Miyagishima's testimony got back to the Japanese barracks, Miyagishima was shunned by the other Japanese. Gizo Oikawa, a Japanese detainee, acknowledged that when Miyagishima returned to the barracks he (Oikawa) told Miyagishima he should "leave the camp and not stay here with the other Japanese." Questioned about the incident by Inspector Bliss, this exchange resulted:

"Where did you expect Miyagishima to go after you told him to get out of the camp, knowing as you are bound to know that all Japanese are detained here?"

"I think that was putting him in a tough spot."

"What do you mean?"

"Well, if I, myself, was in that spot that Miyagishima is, I would kill myself."[5]

Four days after his first hearing, Miyagishima asked to correct his statements and was once again brought before the immigration inspectors. In this second hearing he said he had lived continuously in the United States since 1922 and had never married. On February 20 he had testified that his brother Umeo had four children, Takashi, Fusaye, Kazue and Yukie, but on February 24 he said his brother had no children.

"Where did you get those names from if they aren't your brother's children?" Inspector Herstrom asked.

"I just got them out of my head," he answered.

Nearly every statement Miyagishima made on February 20 he contradicted in a similar way when he testified on February 24.[6]

It was this kind of testimony that angered the immigration inspectors. Still, they denied that their anger was exhibited in any manner other than by occasionally raising their voices.

Walter S. Bliss, who supervised the team of immigration inspectors, was so incensed by the investigation into the inspectors' conduct that he wrote a letter to W. Kelly, chief supervisor of the Immigration and Naturalization Service Border Patrol, asking for a personal interview to air his side of the matter. Bliss felt the investigators just did not understand the conditions under which the immigration inspectors had to work. "From the first day at the Missoula camp there was among the Japanese an atmosphere of intrigue and personal animosity against us, which became progressively apparent in the handling of investigations," he wrote. Bliss said the Japanese in the camp encouraged one another to lie to the inspectors and ostracized those who told the truth. He claimed the charges against him were the work of enemies of the United States, aimed at removing him from his job because he was so effective at getting the truth out of the Japanese. He wrote to Kelly:

"Development of the situation which has come about was anticipated by us, and it is but a logical result of the scheming on the part of the enemy element in preponderance at the camp, and, sensing that it was coming, I acquired certain vital information in the camp, which considered in light of previous long experience on Japanese work, completes a full picture of the situation which has developed, and the allegations which must have been made, all a part of the plan conceived and carried out by the element mentioned."[7]

Bliss said the "situation was so peculiar and the activities of the principal disturbing element in the camp so secretly insidious" that it was impossible to adequately describe them in writing. He explained to Kelly that the Japanese were trying to stir up trouble for the American government and for the immigration inspectors "without any one of us having in the least been at fault."

He was obsessed with the idea that the Japanese were bent on thwarting his investigations into their alien status. In another memo answering the charges against him, he said when he arrived at Fort Missoula he discovered "the so-called Japanese big shots of Los Angeles and Southern California had been sent to this camp." He named among these Shungo Abe, Shinn Shibata, Gongora Nakamura and a Japanese he identified only as Muto. Many of these men, he said, were attorneys or runners for attorneys who "made their living entirely by coaching, teaching and representing illegal entrant Japanese."[8]

He said the day after he arrived in camp the Japanese held a mass meeting at which it was decided everything possible would be done by the Japanese to get him fired. He said an informant kept him posted on these activities, including a requirement by the Japanese camp "mayor," Yahei Taoka, that any Japanese summoned for questioning would first have to see the mayor for instructions on how to testify. Records at the National Archives show the informant Bliss relied on was Ito Yenkichi of Santa Cruz, California.[9] Yenkichi liked very little about what he said went on in the Japanese compound and complained to the immigration inspectors bitterly about it. But what he could not abide more than anything was that Taoka was mayor and he was not.

"Why should the officers here allow the Japanese detained to be represented by a Japanese who has only been in the United States three or four years instead of some Japanese who has resided in the United States 30 years or longer and has a family, born and living in the United States.

This man, Taoka, has no real interest in this country. . . ."[10] Of course, Yenichi had lived in America since early in the century. He said he had "raised all of my children American way and we never use any Japanese language in my home."

Yenichi thought most of the Japanese at Fort Missoula were disloyal to America and were allowed too many privileges at the camp:

"Morning and night we are more free really than outside. We have all kinds of newspapers—all Japanese and others. Every time the news broadcasts over the radio comes on wherein Japanese have scored a victory, all the Japanese in this camp are very proud. Then not only in the barracks but in all of them, they have quite a celebration, dancing and loud talking. This makes my stomach sick and every time they do this, I go to the bathroom to get away from the rejoicing."[11]

Yenkichi was very eager to assure the inspectors that he was loyal to America and would do anything for them.

Others were not so cooperative. Bliss told his superiors that it was "hardly possible to set forth in words the tremendous opposition encountered by us in attempting to perform our official duties at Fort Missoula, Montana." That opposition came not only from the Japanese, he implied, but also from others in the Immigration Service.[12] One of those who created this opposition, he charged, though not mentioning him by name, was Herman F. Schwandt, the man whose report triggered the investigation. Bliss hoped to discredit Schwandt by showing that his allegations about the conduct of the immigration inspectors were motivated by revenge.

One day a trainload of about 155 Japanese arrived in Missoula from Seattle. Bliss said the immigration officer who accompanied the Seattle Japanese, whom he identified only as "the Inspector in Charge at Seattle," an obvious reference to Schwandt, informed him that "there was no necessity of our even contemplating questioning any of this Seattle bunch as he personally had investigated each individual before leaving Seattle and had caused to be taken from the group all those who were 'wet' [illegal aliens] and had left them in the Seattle station."[13]

Bliss related further that "merely as a matter of curiosity" he looked over the first fifty men and "at once recognized three whom we had photographs of showing that they were unlawfully in the United States." Bliss said he immediately questioned three or four of the men and the first two "readily 'broke', admitting they were bond jumpers, unlawfully in the United States." He said all this happened within an hour of his meeting with Schwandt:

"Sincerely, without any thought of embarrassment to him, I brought these facts to his attention and told him that after sixteen years of experience, I personally would never make a statement to anybody that any group of Japanese that I had investigated did not contain some who possibly were unlawfully in the United States."[14]

Bliss claimed Schwandt had previously told the head office that none of these Japanese was an illegal alien, and the embarrassment this caused Schwandt resulted in him feeling "very bitter toward us" even though Bliss said it was not his "intention in any way to embarrass any other immigration officer."

Bliss also had an answer for the reports of shouting and physical abuse that were surfacing. He said Japanese informants were worried that other Japanese were suspicious of them so he called several Japanese, including Mayor Yahei Taoka, into the area where immigration questioning took place and had them sit outside the door. He proceeded to bring in the informers and "make a lot of noise and knock over a chair and hammer the walls and desk," he said. At one point one of the informers threw a pipe under the wall partition that separated him from the Japanese outside, then "put one foot out as if he were knocked to the floor and mussed up his hair and twisted the collar of his blouse," Bliss said. He admitted that on occasion the inspectors would raise their voices or hammer on the desks, "but never at any time did any of us lay a hand on any Japanese alien of [sic] physically mistreat them in any way."

While he conceded to having raised his voice, he said he never swore at the men. "I have lots of faults," he said, "but I don't use profanity."[15]

Bliss said the inspectors showed remarkable restraint even when their lives were threatened. During questioning as part of the investigation into the alleged mistreatment, Bliss said one Japanese, whom he identified only as Sato, was making threats against him. (There were at least six Japanese with the last name of Sato at Fort Missoula.) Bliss said he sent for Sato and discovered a knife hidden in his clothing. Even this seemed of little concern to Bliss, judging by his testimony. There is no record that this landed Sato in the guardhouse. Bliss said only that his reaction to discovering the knife was the comment that Sato "just wasn't brave enough to carry on [sic] his threats."[16]

One of the lesser allegations made about the inspectors was that they required the Japanese to stand for hour after hour, either waiting for their hearings to begin or while being questioned by the inspectors. Bliss acknowledged at one point that some were made to stand "for several hours,"[17] but later said that "at no time, during any questioning by me of any Japanese alien in this camp, did I require that alien to remain standing for any extended period of time."[18]

Clyde Neu, a supply officer at Fort Missoula while the Japanese were detained, said he personally was aware that some men were being abused. "I knew they were mistreating some of them," he said. "God, I'd hear 'em slap these Japanese and one thing and another."[19]

Neu remembers the inspectors making the Japanese stand for long periods, and it is his recollection that they were kept standing outside even in freezing weather. One day, when the temperature was thirty degrees below zero, Neu said, an "old fellow" was told to appear for a hearing. "You be here at 9 o'clock in the morning," Neu said the man was ordered. "So he'd be there. They'd say, 'Well, you just stay outside there until we call you.' He'd be out there in the cold."

Neu testified during the inquiry in 1942 that the man "would be there all day and not called in. He would be their [sic] the next morning again."[20]

Most of the employees at Fort Missoula who worked in or near the building in which the Japanese were questioned by the immigration inspectors were interviewed in connection with the investigation. The great majority of that testimony suggests that physical abuse was rare but verbal abuse was routine. The employees accepted it as part of the inspectors' job.

Clarence V. Carlson was a patrol inspector attached to the Spokane district but assigned to Fort Missoula from December 16, 1941, through April 30, 1942. He said he saw some mistreatment.

"I had seen them, [Tai Hoon] Kim [a Korean interpreter] in particular, would take his forefingers and push the alien in the shoulders and chest to make them tell the truth and the Inspectors would take the aliens [sic] clothing and wrap it tightly around the neck, not tightly, [sic] in order to threaten actual abuse."

Carlson said he saw Kim do that "on several occasions" but did not report it because "it was my understanding that the Inspectors were there to handle that business and [were] not under the jurisdiction of this camp." He said the inspectors would push the Japanese against the wall "merely to emphasize the questions," frequently called them "yellow-bellied cowards" and "liars" and regularly pounded on the table. He corroborated Rinzo Saito's testimony that he stood for long periods, saying he saw Saito "stand in the building there for I should say three or four days at least, practically eight hours a day." He said others also had to stand for days but he did not know their names. [21]

Guard Leonard Kuka said he never saw any Japanese hit but he heard some verbal abuse. "Well, just once or twice they were called 'dirty, lying and yellow,'" he said. "That was all I heard." [22]

John Harrington, a postal inspector who worked in the building where the Japanese were questioned, said the inspectors raised their voices frequently. "They seemed to think the Japanese were lying to them quite consistently," he said. [23]

Thomas Bayles, a patrol inspector at the fort, said the more he heard what went on during the hearings the more his sympathies shifted from the Japanese to the inspectors.

"I thought, at first, it was considerable abuse being given verbally to the Japanese but during the month I worked there, I became more of the opinion that, although the talk was loud and there was some stomping of feet and hitting on a table which some alien or outsider might perhaps think abusive, it really wasn't actual abuse to the detainees . . . I believe entirely the situation of loud talk was caused . . . by bald-faced lying on the part of those being investigated," he said. [24]

For example, Bayles said, one alien gave different names for both his birthplace and his mother. "When questioned, said he had two mothers and had been born in two different places," Bayles recounted.

Bayles said he thought at times the inspectors were unnecessarily abusing the Japanese "although it wasn't incumbent upon me to investigate the matter." He talked to the inspectors and said he "found it a practise [sic] which resulted in getting the truth" and showing the aliens "they would not tolerate being lied to." The yelling and stomping "was merely a procedure to catch them in a lie or let them know that they had found to be lying," he concluded. He ultimately decided it was justified because "some bald-faced lying by aliens under investigation . . . would make the most polite church-going man we have yell and stomp his feet." [25]

During the course of the Missoula inquiry, investigators learned of allegations of abuse at Fort Lincoln, North Dakota, where the same team of Immigration Service inspectors questioned Japanese after they finished work in Missoula. At Fort Lincoln, Otasaburou Sumi had two teeth knocked out by interpreter Edward Pai during questioning by Bliss and Brown.[26]

At the conclusion of the investigation, the Justice Department ordered interpreters Edward Pai and Chai Hoon Kim fired, citing evidence that they had struck the Japanese. It determined that Immigrant Inspector Walter S. Bliss, Special Inspector Martin H. Herstrom Jr. and Patrol Inspector Harold W. Brown were guilty of pushing, shaking and shouting at the Japanese, making them stand for long periods and confining them to the guardhouse without adequate reason for periods ranging from one to twenty-seven days. The three were suspended from duty on July 17, 1942. Immigration Service Commissioner Earl G. Harrison said in determining their punishment he took into account the fact the men had no other blemishes on their records and their "misguided zeal" could be attributed to the fact the alien hearings "took place shortly after this country had been attacked by Japanese forces and while battles were still raging in the Pacific. . . ."[27]

Harrison also concluded that in fairness it was important to note that some of the Japanese adopted "defiant and obstructive tactics."

The officers' suspension from duty without pay lasted for 90 days. In addition, Herstrom was demoted from special inspector to immigrant inspector. Harrison said firing would be too severe a punishment, given the men's long and satisfactory service. He said the loss of salary plus "the mental punishment which the officers have undoubtedly already suffered by reason of the uncertainty as to the outcome of the charges" would be a deterrent to future misconduct.

Though the investigation was secret it could not be kept entirely quiet because many Missoulians employed at the camp were interviewed as to their knowledge of what had happened. Though nothing was ever released officially, the goings-on were apparently grist for the Missoula rumor mill. State Sen. John Campbell was incensed over what he viewed as this "glaring miscarriage of justice" accorded the inspectors and wrote U.S. Sen. Burton K. Wheeler to ask him to intervene.[28]

Wheeler asked Attorney General Francis Biddle to look into the matter. "People of Montana are very much aroused . . . ," he wrote Biddle. There is no record of Biddle's response, but the investigation continued without interruption and two months after Wheeler's appeal it was concluded with Harrison's recommendations.

The Labor Shortage: Hate the Jap, But Use Him

B Y LATE SPRING of 1942 hearings before both the Alien Enemy Hearing Boards and the Immigration and Naturalization Service inspectors were completed for the thousand Japanese. The fact that the government believed it had made determinations as to the loyalty and alien status of the Japanese, coupled with President Roosevelt's decision to move all West Coast Japanese inland, meant many of the Japanese were transferred from Fort Missoula. Roosevelt had given authority to the Army to exclude any person from the Western Defense Command, the military designation for an area encompassing roughly the western half of the states of Washington, Oregon and California. Lt. Gen. John DeWitt, commander of that military zone, ordered all persons of Japanese ancestry relocated from that area. They were sent to one of ten detention camps established by the War Relocation Authority. By early summer of 1942 the Fort Missoula Japanese began an exodus that for some led to a reunion with their families at a War Relocation Authority camp and for others meant transfer to another Immigration Service detention compound.[1]

A large contingent was sent to Fort Sill, Oklahoma, another of the alien detention camps operated by the Immigration and Naturalization Service. Among those was Yahei Taoka, the man who had served as "mayor" of the Fort Missoula Japanese. A month after his transfer to Fort Sill, Taoka wrote to Supervisor Nick Collaer to report on "the boys from Fort Missoula."[2]

> Dear Mr. Collaer,
> How are you, Sir? I guess you are working just like a Trojan these days. It seems only yesterday we bade adieu to you at the station and I cannot believe already one month has elapsed since we arrived here. In this brief intervening period, a number of incidents have happened—I regret I cannot give you any report here—which has kept me pretty well occupied. However, one pleasing fact is that all the boys from Ft. Missoula are in excellent health although we all miss dear old Missoula very much. I was very pleased to hear that quite a number of San Francisco boys at yours [sic] have since been released to join their respective families. I also hear that a great work is now going on in the camp with a view to beautification of the whole area i.e. transplanting of trees, preparation of the swimming pool etc.
> The latest news, so far as we are concerned is that we are to move to yet another quarter very shortly, possibly down South.
> Please let me thank you once again for all the kindnesses you extended to me whilst at yours [sic] and please remember me to Mr. McLaughlin and Mr. Beckstrom.
>
> Sincerely yours,
Y. Taoka

A labor shortage meant many Italians were pressed into service harvesting sugar beets. Immigration Service officer Bert Fraser, right, checks the progress of the workers. MONTANA HISTORICAL SOCIETY COLLECTION

Taoka was obviously quite pleased with his treatment at Fort Missoula. Another indication of what it was like was recorded by Jerre Mangione, a government official who visited all the immigration service camps. When Mangione got to Missoula he said Collaer advised him to talk with Taoka.

" . . . I tried to interview the man whom the Japanese had elected as their mayor but was told by one of his assistants that the mayor was on vacation. 'And how is he spending his vacation?' I asked, certain he must be joking. But the assistant was perfectly serious; the mayor, he explained, was spending most of it on the miniature golf course the Japanese had built in the camp. The assistant was willing to take me to his chief but requested I desist from discussing camp business with him since he had been working hard for many months and deserved a complete rest from his duties. When we reached the golf course the assistant pointed him out to me and offered to introduce us, but the mayor seemed so immersed in the game that I decided not to disturb his concentration and postponed my meeting with him until he had returned from his vacation."[3]

Not long after that incident, most of the Japanese were sent to other camps. And just as the Japanese were saying goodbye to Montana, so were thousands of soldiers, off to combat in Europe or the Pacific. Montana sent 57,000 men—10 percent of its population—into military service. This exodus created a manpower shortage that plagued the agriculture industry in the state so severely that for months farmers and sugar beet processors pleaded for the return of interned Japanese to Montana so that they could work in the fields. Ironically, this came at the same time as some Montanans were trying to keep Japanese-American university students out of the state.

When it first became apparent that a labor shortage was imminent, some employers went to unusual extremes to find laborers. Arthur Deschamps, who was in charge of operations in the Missoula Valley for the American Crystal Sugar Co., said he made a trip to Spokane where he recruited transients along Trent Avenue. After putting those recruits to work in Montana sugar beet fields, he soon discarded that idea because he said most of the men were alcoholics and couldn't be counted on to do the job.[4] When that plan proved useless, Deschamps went to California internment camps in search of laborers. He had some success, but it wasn't the number of workers he enlisted that would leave a lasting impression on him.

"The sight that I saw there really stayed in my mind," he recalled. "I guess that I will know [it] for the rest of my life. [What I saw] was here was this spectacle of American citizens behind barbed wire being guarded by guards in uniform. A little group of Boy Scouts who were at that time in the camps were parading within the campground with their scout banner and their little uniforms and the American flag. The contradiction of that spectacle was so seemingly bizarre that I just never forgot it."[5]

Deschamps said as a result of his efforts, about 25 Japanese came to Missoula to work. It wasn't an altogether smooth venture. "The emotion that that generated locally was beyond really any semblance of common sense," Deschamps said. For example, before he introduced Japanese laborers into the Bitterroot Valley, he held a meeting with the townspeople in Hamilton to discuss it.

"Well, I'll tell you something," he said. "There were a number of people in the Hamilton area who were going to do whatever they could to disrupt this. They were not about to allow these enemies of the country to come into their community."[6]

These ill feelings toward any person of Japanese ancestry mirrored those of officials at the highest levels of state government. Responding to an inquiry from Representative John Tolan, the former Montanan who was serving as chairman of the House Committee Investigating National Defense Migration, as to whether Montana would accept Japanese laborers, Gov. Sam Ford wired this telegram: "From information received, opinion here opposed to importation of enemy aliens into Montana to be used as agricultural workers."[7]

But as pressure increased to get behind the war effort, Montana beet farmers raised production quotas to alleviate the sugar shortage that had resulted in rationing. In 1941 the state sugar beet crop yielded 2.5 million 100-pound bags of sugar, a sufficient quantity under rationing restrictions for more than 10 million Americans. In setting crop levels for the 1942 growing season, Montana farmers displayed the same zeal state residents were to exhibit in setting national records for war bond sales. (Montanans oversubscribed to eight war bond drives. In Missoula, when the call was sounded for scrap metal donations, the citizenry mobilized so effectively that some residents convinced the county government to donate to the effort a Civil War cannon that was on display on the courthouse lawn.) In 1942 sugar beet farmers raised production levels as high as 25 percent in some counties. That meant 86,000 acres of beets needed seeding, thinning, topping and harvesting.[8]

Montana historian Dave Walter, in a 1987 article in *Montana Magazine*, sketched the picture faced by many Montana farmers as typified by conditions in Phillips County. By early March 1942 nearly a thousand men from that county had been inducted into the armed forces, and another thousand had left to work in war-materials industries on the West Coast. At the same time, Walter said, beet producers had contracted to seed a crop 25 percent larger than the 1941 harvest. On this issue the *Phillips County News* took an editorial stand that reflected many Montanans' attitudes regarding the employment of Japanese laborers:

"Most of us are agreed these days that we should glance at our war situation with realism. . . . If that stand has any foundation at all, then why not extend it to the question of moving Japanese nationals and naturalized citizens into the Great Plains area from the potential combat zones and military bases of the Far West?

"Newspapers of the area have, with one accord, jumped all over the proposal to send these people here. The words have been different, but the music has been the same—WE DON'T WANT 'EM! . . . But why isn't it sensible to ship them to sparsely populated areas where they can be watched closely, where defense industries are few, and where army and navy drafts are making serious inroads on the labor supply? . . . As we see it, it is possible to hate the innards of every Jap ever born and still make use of them. The United States is widely reputed to be a practical nation and, as we view the matter, this is an excellent time to demonstrate it. Hate the Jap, if you will, but also admit that he is a good worker, a natural farmer, and a human commodity which this region is going to need if it is to continue as a substantial supplier to the war effort."[9]

Within weeks, Gov. Ford and others had come around to that position. The governor announced on March 13 that Montana farmers had done an abrupt "about face" and now wanted Japanese laborers. Many wanted them only under rigid conditions. In an interview in April with the *Great Falls Tribune*, Gov. Ford outlined those restrictions:

"If they are brought in they should be kept under guard. So many have left to defend the country and there is no way of knowing American-born Japanese or loyal ones from others. When casualty lists start coming in with names of Montanans on it, I fear for the safety of any Jap in this state. The army has provided proper protection. Any violence or direct action would be most unfortunate and might result in retaliation by Japs toward American-held prisoners. This seems to be one important fundamental point to be considered.

"We are justified in assuming that with the close of the war, the coastal states, especially will use every means possible to prevent the return of Japanese evacuees. They have learned the bitter lesson."[10]

Ford wanted assurances from the War Department that the Japanese would be removed from Montana after the war and he pleaded with Montanans to refuse to sell their land to any Japanese-Americans. He said Montanans couldn't compete with the Japanese when it came to farming and if Asians were allowed permanent residency "the white man will be driven from our fertile farms."[11]

Once Montanans became more receptive to Japanese farm labor, they found it wasn't so simple to secure as they had imagined. First there was government permission to obtain, and that accomplished, the Japanese had to be persuaded it was to their benefit to leave the camps to perform menial labor. In trying to arrange potential laborers' release from camps, beet growers enlisted the aid of the state's congressmen. In a wire to Senator Burton K. Wheeler, the Northern Montana Beet Growers Association expressed its members' frustration over unproductive attempts to find laborers:

"We have exhausted every means available to us to get sugar beet field labor. . . . Financial ruin face [sic] the beet growers in our area. We request you state our case to the president in effort to have company of US soldiers designated to Montana beet areas for guard and patrol duty for Japanese evacuees[.] Also assurance these people will be moved from Montana at end of war in accordance with governor's request. . . . Quick action necessary if crop is to be saved."[12]

Montana's other senator, James Murray, also attempted to influence the federal government to cut the red tape that kept the Japanese in War Relocation Authority camps. He even wrote to Roosevelt's secretary, M.H. McIntyre, asking him to use his influence to get a WRA camp in Montana, and complaining that his attempts had been rebuffed.

"Dear Mac: I have been trying to get a war relocation center established in Montana but nothing has been done. If Senator Wheeler had asked for it, probably he would have gotten it; but these agencies around here seem to pay no attention to my requests. . . . We have got all these Jap evacuees, but the Employment Service under McNutt has failed to get them out on the farms."[13]

Burton K. Wheeler
MONTANA HISTORICAL
SOCIETY COLLECTION

Though no WRA camps were established in Montana, the federal government did review possible locations before dismissing the idea. A memorandum in the Fort Missoula files at the National Archives reveals that two locations were considered. Jardine in Park County was suggested as ideal for a detention camp for 10,000 to 20,000 people. It was surrounded on three sides by mountains, "making escape impossible." The other site was Wild Horse Island at Flathead Lake. This four-square-mile piece of land was projected as being able to accommodate 50 to 100 people. No mention was made in this unsigned memo as to the logistics of getting laborers to and from the island.[14]

When importation of Japanese labor was finally permitted, it met with mixed success. Arthur Deschamps said the Japanese whom he found work for did excellent jobs. He particularly remembers one worker who, before the war, had owned a theater in Stockton, California. This man brought his wife and three children, aged 4 to 9, to work on a farm near Clinton, where they lived in a log cabin. They were supervised by a man named Elliott, Deschamps recalled. On November 1, 1942, the crop was not fully harvested but it had begun to snow and Elliott told the laborers he expected them to stop working. Deschamps said the Japanese reaction was astonishing:

" 'No, Mr. Elliott,' they said. 'We'll stay. We'll work. We'll stay here just as long as you let us. We'll work just as long as we can get out in the field.'

"Well their ambition and their determination to get the work, [get] the rest of the beets, was almost beyond imagination. . . . They were just really wonderful people. I shall never forget them."[15]

Another Japanese couple, Jeanette and Harry Kawaguchi, came to Townsend to work thinning and topping beets on the Harold Marks farm. In 1968 Marks told University of Montana journalism student Donald Wright that Jeanette Kawaguchi "had been the personal maid to a Hollywood movie star" and Harry Kawaguchi "had been running a men's clothing store in Los Angeles" before being sent to relocation camps, which "they called concentration camps."[16]

(Controversy over what to call the camps that housed the Japanese in the United States was persistent. On July 28, 1943, Nick Collaer, the supervisor at the Fort Missoula camp, who by then had been promoted to chief of the Detention and Deportation Section of the Immigration Service, wrote a memo to W. Kelly, assistant commissioner for Alien Control, in which he complained that some "Central Office officials and district directors" had been referring to the camps as "concentration camps." "I don't know how this expression effects you, but to me, the words 'concentration camp' has a definite connotation of injustice which I will not conceive applies to our facilities." Nearly 40 years later the dispute still simmered. The Commission on Wartime Relocation and Internment of Civilians, in its Congressionally authorized report, "Personal Justice Denied," noted that critics had charged that use of any term other than "concentration camps" was a euphemism. The commission concluded that given the atrocities committed by the Nazis in the World War II death camps, the phrase had come to have very different meanings. Thus, while

Efforts to get Japanese from the War Relocation Authority camps in other states to come to Montana to harvest sugar beets were not particularly successful. However, Italians from Fort Missoula worked in the area. One man takes a break from lunch to form a "V" for victory with a pair of sugar beets.
MONTANA HISTORICAL SOCIETY COLLECTION

the United States camps were "bleak and bare, and life in them had many hardships, . . . they were not extermination camps, nor did the American government embrace a policy of torture or liquidation of the ethnic Japanese." For reasons of accuracy and fairness, the commission said, its report would call them relocation camps.)

The Kawaguchis were two of eight Japanese working on the Marks farm. Mrs. Marks said prejudice against those Japanese was widespread. They were not allowed in the Townsend movie theater and local barbers refused to cut their hair. The prejudice extended even to the government. Jeanette Kawaguchi tried to enlist in the Women's Army Air Corps but was rejected on the grounds that she had pulmonary tuberculosis. Mrs. Marks said what particularly disappointed Jeanette Kawaguchi was the local doctors could find no trace of tuberculosis.

Montana farmers asked for 5,000 Japanese laborers.[17] They were to get only a fraction of that number. The monetary incentives were not attractive to many Japanese who had owned their own farms or businesses before the war. Beet growers were offering the following wages:

Blocking and thinning	$10 an acre
Hoeing	$3.50 an acre
Second hoeing	$2.50 an acre
Pulling and topping	$1.05 a ton, up to 12 tons, then 95 cents a ton

When the government was slow to react to beet growers' demands for labor and Japanese were slow to volunteer, the Northern Montana Beetgrowers threatened to plow under the beet crops.[18] In late May a "token force" of Japanese arrived from Washington State to inspect conditions in the fields. After a few days the 13 men were said to have "sent a favorable report to countrymen at the Federal reception center at Puyallup, Wash." As a result, farmers anticipated "several hundred" Japanese would come to the state for field work.[19]

By June 17, 1942, 231 Japanese were working on Montana farms. More were expected every day. The influx soon dwindled to a trickle, however, when the Japanese found conditions were not always as promised. When only 65 Japanese from Fort Missoula volunteered, there were grumblings sounded to the effect that the internees should be required to do the work. But Frank Cleland, manager of the American Crystal Sugar Company's Missoula processing plant, said only those who volunteered would be used. Cleland was talking more than just good sense. Sixty-three percent of the Japanese in relocation centers were American citizens and federal laws did not permit Americans to be drafted for work against their will. Additionally, a United States-Japanese agreement that extended the Geneva Conventions of 1929 to civilian, as well as military, internees, prohibited forced labor of aliens. Cleland said farmers who employed the Japanese were "surprised and pleased" at their skill but the Japanese were not always pleased with their working conditions. Cleland told the *Missoulian* that "the Japanese resented the fact they were not granted liberties which were promised when they came to Montana. . . ." He did not elaborate.[20]

However, the manner in which the Japanese who came to the Bitterroot Valley were treated is testimony to why some might have been dis-

Italian crews were sent to work in the national forests. These men labored in the Idaho panhandle.
U.S. FOREST SERVICE

illusioned. Only those Japanese who were born in the United States—in other words, American citizens—were permitted to work outside the internment camps. Yet, in Ravalli County, labor camps set up in Stevensville and Corvallis were policed by armed guards. The county sheriff appointed Clarence Hagen and Arbury Watson to patrol the compounds.[21]

Bitterrooters were encouraged in these tactics by Gov. Sam Ford. In an October 9 speech to the Hamilton Chamber of Commerce, Ford said the Japanese laborers should be treated well "but not pampered." He also declared that the government should adopt "a strict policy regarding the Japanese" and put pressure on the second and third generation Japanese to "get behind the war effort."[22]

Once the farmers had moderate success in importing labor, others tried to follow their lead. The Northern Pacific hired 60 Japanese to work on the railroad. They worked in one group, segregated from other employees. Their presence created unrest, however, as the *Missoulian* reported that residents of what it described only as a "western Montana town" had begun to "agitate for removal of the aliens and produced pressure that may force the Northern Pacific to send the Japs away."[23]

The number of Japanese at Fort Missoula had dwindled by the close of 1942 when only 29 Japanese remained there. There were still 1,200 Italians, however, and soon they were courted by a variety of employers. The federal government recruited 360 for work in the Forest Service. By July 1, 1943, 180 Italians were employed in the Kaniksu Forest, 35 in the Coeur d'Alene, 61 in the Clearwater and 84 in the Kootenai Forest. It was a successful undertaking. Only one of the 360 asked to return to Fort Missoula.[24]

These Fort Missoula residents took a job doing road work. They are headed for the Pierce, Idaho, area.
U.S. FOREST SERVICE

Unlike the Japanese field laborers, these Italians were welcomed into the communities without hesitation. Their reception was ironic because all of them were Italian nationals, citizens of a nation with which the United States was at war. In contrast, the only Japanese employed in Montana were American citizens, but they were frequently treated as if they were enemies.

The Italians seemed to harbor no ill feelings about their confinement. In fact, they were eager to please. The *Missoulian* told one story about members of an Italian forest crew that proved themselves good Samaritans.

"A group of internees encountered an overturned truck on the North Idaho road. They stopped, righted the truck, and mechanics among them took it apart. Finding a bent axle, they built a fire by the road, heated the axle, straightened it, and returned the truck to service. The wood hauler offer $10 in compensation, but the internees declined to accept any payment."[25]

One Forest Service crew on its own time shingled the roof of the Catholic Church in Priest River, Idaho, and the Coeur d'Alene crew built a caretaker's house to adjoin the Kiwanis Club's home for underprivileged children. The Italians even made speaking engagements at service clubs in Coeur d'Alene, Sandpoint, Newport and Priest River.[26]

By the end of July 1943, 800 of 1,300 Italians at Fort Missoula had received work parole. Not only were they employed by the Forest Service, but the Northern Pacific, Great Northern and Milwaukee railroads attracted many of the men. In Missoula two of the men were employed as chefs at the Florence Hotel and others worked as maids and busboys.

St. Patrick Hospital used others as orderlies and townspeople employed a few as gardeners.[27]

Immigration Service Commissioner Earl Harrison visited Fort Missoula in July 1943 and, in an interview with the *Missoulian*, explained that it was the goal of the government to release the Italians "as rapidly and consistently as the internal security of the country justifies." He said hearings had been held for each of the Italians and none had been released on work parole without clearance from the Federal Bureau of Investigation. The camp officials had never had trouble with the men, Harrison said, as there had been general cooperation among them and no escape attempts. "As for the detainees, they generally want to see Italy get out of the war," he declared.[28]

The *Missoulian* followed up Harrison's glowing interview about the demeanor of the Fort Missoula Italians with an editorial that summarized what it said were Americans' feelings toward the Italians:

"One thing will ever remain a strange characteristic of World War II, namely the continued friendliness of the American people for the Italian people throughout Mussolini's period of mastery. There has been no hate manifested toward the Italian people and there is not the slightest desire to punish the Italian people for the misdeeds of their criminal leaders. . . . Americans have not come to hate the Italians. . . . They still remember

Truckloads of seamen head for the "outing camp" near Fort Missoula. From that base they worked on labor crews.
MONTANA HISTORICAL SOCIETY COLLECTION

Several romances developed between the Italians at the fort and Missoula-area women. Here, Mario Cananero poses with an admirer outside the Recreation Center. In May 1945 dozens of women stood on the Northern Pacific platform and wept as a train left for New York, carrying the remaining Italians from Fort Missoula who were being repatriated to Italy.

MANSFIELD LIBRARY COLLECTION, UNIVERSITY OF MONTANA

the Italians as the frugal, happy, hard-working folk they had known before—and as lovers of peace.[29]

Two months later Italy surrendered. The *Missoulian* reported the Italians working in town were "overjoyed" to be out of the war. "Surely this will mean that I will be able to see my mother that much sooner," one was quoted as saying. Others were pessimistic that there would be jobs in Italy to return to and one volunteered that he would prefer to stay in Missoula.[30]

It was the beginning of the end of the Fort Missoula Alien Detention Camp. Oddly enough, 258 Japanese were transferred to the camp late in 1943 but were sent to a Santa Fe, New Mexico, camp in March 1944. A few of the Italians joined the United States Army and were thus permitted to remain in this country after the war. Most, however, were transferred to Ellis Island and repatriated to their homeland on either the *S.S. Gripsholm* or the *S.D. Drottningholm*.[31]

AFTERWORD

O<small>N</small> J<small>ULY</small> 1, 1944, the Immigration Service officially closed the Fort Missoula camp and returned it to the United States Army, ending a provocative, and sometimes inglorious, chapter in Missoula history.

For the Italians, who had been brought to the fort when their damaged ships were seized by U.S. authorities, and who were unable to secure passage home while the world was at war, it had not been an oppressive episode. Their life at Fort Missoula, while not ideal, was without real hardship. They were far from home, but most of the men were seafarers, not unused to long separations from family and fatherland. Their treatment at the camp was humane. In fact, life for most was surely better in several respects than what they knew in Italy. Many were no doubt relieved to be distanced from a war for which they felt no fervor, though thoughts of family and friends enduring life in a war-torn country must have filled many hours. There is no evidence that either the camp officers or guards harbored animosity toward the Italians for their country's alliance with the Axis. The townspeople welcomed their presence at the fort, frequently attending concerts and plays presented by the men. When the Immigration Service gave permission for the Italians to work outside the fort, not a voice was heard in opposition. These were people not unlike Missoulians themselves. Their appearance, customs, culture and religion were familiar. By 1941, Missoula was already home to a number of Italians who had immigrated to the United States, many of whom had found jobs with the railroad.

The housing of a thousand Italian citizens at an abandoned Army fort outside the city was an event worth notice for most Missoulians, but not a development that stirred fear or hatred in the town.

The Japanese experience at the fort differed in several respects. There was no disagreement as to why the Italians were interned. But why were the Japanese detained? They were arrested without charge and isolated in a deserted Army camp hundreds of miles from their homes for reasons most would never understand and the government would never disclose.

Was it a crime to be an alien? Oriental exclusion laws barred them from citizenship, so they had no opportunity to publicly swear allegiance to the United States. They could not forswear allegiance to Japan because they would then be left as men without a country. What had they done? Because the United States Department of Justice claims no knowledge as to where loyalty hearing records are stored, there is no evidence either that these men were loyal or had schemes for sabotage. What the evidence does show is that many were arrested because the government thought they were the most influential members of the Japanese community in the states. The United States government had, in effect, made success a crime.

Once the Japanese reached Fort Missoula, all evidence suggests that the vast majority were treated well. Camp supervisor Nick Collaer deserves high praise for that. He made it clear at every opportunity, both inside and outside the camp, that the Italians and Japanese at the fort had committed no crime and were primarily victims of circumstance. Collaer's single failing was that he did not ride herd sufficiently on the Immigration Service inspectors who came from the West Coast to interrogate those aliens they suspected had entered the country illegally. It resulted in the one black mark that would tarnish the operation of the camp.

The Immigration Service inspectors' routine task for many years before the war had been to question suspected illegal aliens. They did so with a firmness they thought appropriate to get them to the truth. Unfortunately, that authoritarian attitude led to outright abuse when the inspectors grilled men from a nation that had just dealt a crushing blow to American naval forces. What the inspectors failed to understand was that with United States' entry into the war they were laboring under a new set of regulations. These men were no longer just aliens. They were civilian citizens of a hostile nation and harsh treatment was proscribed by the rules of the Geneva Conventions. The rough treatment of the Japanese, when revealed, caused ripples of apprehension throughout the administration in Washington. It was all the excuse Japan might need, government officials thought, to badly treat those Americans held in Nippon prison camps. Ironically, while word apparently never reached Japan, that country needed no excuse to commit uncounted atrocities against American soldiers in their hands.

The attitude of the townspeople toward the Japanese is not easily documented. The Japanese had little of the contact with Missoulians that the Italians were afforded. Their presence at the fort, while not a secret, was not likely often on the minds of most Missoulians, who seldom, if ever, got so much as a look at the men. But a glimpse into some Missoulians' frame of mind is suggested by the panic some groups and individuals generated at the suggestion that a few Japanese college students —all of whom were Americans—be allowed to attend the university in Missoula. So much pressure was exerted that, though Montana State University President Ernest O. Melby persevered, the idea finally died.

It would be easy to extrapolate a general attitude from individual incidents. But would it be fair or accurate? Surely some Missoulians hated any Japanese. But evidence also exists to support the thought that others in the town viewed them with respect and did not change their views when the United States went to war against Japan.

In the later years of the camp, some Japanese from Hawaii were interned there briefly. One afternoon, on a supervised visit outside the camp confines, the men walked through a cemetery. They made what they thought was a startling discovery:

"Suddenly someone called out, 'Look, look! How did a Japanese get here?'

"'A Japanese? Buried here? Why, there's another!'

"'And here's one . . .'

"In all, they counted 50 graves of Japanese. They had died between 1900 and 1909, about 30 or 40 years ago. Some had emigrated from Hokkaido and Niigata in northern Japan; others had come from warmer Hiroshima and Wakayama. One had been only 18 when he died, another

Several tombstones at the Missoula City Cemetery mark the graves of Japanese who died in the early 1900s.

19. The majority had been in their 20s and 30s, and a few had been from 59 to 63. The name of the person, his date of birth and death, and his ken — his province — identified the man buried under each tombstone.

"Had they come before the turn of the century to work on the railroads? Why had the 18-year-old and 19-year-old died? Had they not been able to adjust, coming from warm Hiroshima, to work in cold and rugged Montana? What had Montana been like, in the first decade of the 1900s? Had they starved to death? Got caught in an epidemic? Froze during a cold winter? Had the survivors been able to get word to parents in Japan as to what had happened to their beloved sons? Why had so many died in a period of only nine years? Who had provided for these tombs? Was the last Japanese to die also buried here?

"The site of the graves was clean. Someone had mowed the grass, cleared the weeds, and even scrubbed the mold from the tombstones.

"Later, 24 priests received permission from the camp commander to hold Buddhist service for the deceased. They burned incense at each grave. Their tears fell, not for the young men who had died without having their dreams realized, but in gratefulness that the town residents had cared for the graves for so many years, and especially now, knowing the ethnic origin of those buried below.

" 'Those leaders who interned us are Americans,' the priests said. 'But these Missoula residents are Americans too. These Americans are thoughtful enough to care for graves of unknown people. At home, in Hawaii, some children neglect to clean around their own parents' gravesite. And here are Americans who have kept these Japanese tombstones clean.

" 'Yes, the Americans are people with consideration for other human beings. They are human beings first, not Americans or Japanese first.' "[1]

Several Japanese have subsequently visited Missoula to pay their respects at those gravesites at the Missoula City Cemetery, and, in some cases, to hold religious ceremonies. In late October 1994, Masako Kuriyama, the wife of Japan's ambassador to the United States, Takakazu Kuriyama, came to Missoula to view the graves. She was grateful, she said, that when the young men employed by the Northern Pacific Railroad died in the early 1900s, the company fulfilled the immigrants' wishes and printed their tombstones in Japanese. She also speculated as to why so many died so young. Perhaps it was disease, she said, or maybe Montana's harsh winters were too much for them, since most came from southern Japan, where the winters are more forgiving.[2] For whatever reason that these people came to their final rest in ground so far from their homeland, always the visitors express their gratitude to Missoulians who have tended to the graves.

Undoubtedly, not all Montanans have buried their feelings toward Japan for its aggression in World War II, but the state has developed a strong relationship with post-war Japan. Much of the relationship has its roots in former Sen. Mike Mansfield's ties to the country. Mansfield had the longest tenure of any U.S. ambassador to Japan, holding the post from 1977 through 1988, during the terms of both Democratic and Republican presidents. Mansfield has maintained an intense interest in the Pacific Rim since his retirement from public life, working as an adviser on Pacific and East Asian affairs for Goldman, Sachs and Co., an

international investment banking firm. The state government has sought out ties with prefectural governments in Japan, developing a sister-state relationship with Kumamoto. Several cities, including Missoula, have similar relationships with Japanese municipalities. The state maintains trade offices in Japan, which aggressively market Montana products.

The state's education community also has broad and wide-ranging connections with Japan. The University of Montana is the site of the Mansfield Center for Pacific Affairs and the Maureen and Mike Mansfield Center, both of which have Japan as a focal point. Unlike in the days when Montanans fought to keep Japanese-American students from enrolling at the university, today the state's colleges and universities welcome both students and professors from Japan and send their own undergraduates and faculty on exchange programs at Japanese universities.

In 1994, Fort Missoula itself was again in the eye of a storm of controversy. The federal government had turned over to the University of Montana and the state Board of Regents 83 acres of land at the fort, including the area that was the site of the detention camp. The university decided to sell the 83 acres to use the money for academic scholarships. The new owners planned to develop some of the property into a subdivision they named "The Greens at Fort Missoula." What they didn't plan on was the

Many of the barracks were torn down in the early 1950s. Several were moved to the Western Montana Fair in 1954. They are now used as the fair office and agricultural building.
TIM GORDON COLLECTION

uproar that would ensue. In a single week a coalition calling itself "Save the Fort" collected 12,000 signatures of Missoulians who wanted a chance to vote whether to override a zoning decision by the city that would have permitted the development. The question landed on the ballot in June and voters easily overturned the zoning, shelving the developers' dreams for the fort, but preserving at least temporarily the dreams of other Missoulians who want the land left as open space.

Most of the buildings that housed the detention camps are gone. The golf course and recreation fields where the Japanese and Italians engaged in sport have long been overgrown. Several officers' homes still line an attractive, tree-lined street and a museum tells the story of the fort's early days.

Today occasional visitors come to see the place that served as home for men caught up in a conflict they were powerless to control. The wood and concrete that sheltered them have vanished. Perhaps the history of what happened to them here will endure.

INTRODUCTION

1. "History of Fort Missoula," author unknown, found in the Adjutant's Desk at Fort Missoula, Montana, by Capt. E.W. Ely, 4th Infantry, 7 March 1931.

2. Ibid.

CHAPTER ONE

1. Memorandum in re the alien and alien enemy-detention problem, 14 October 1942, National Archives, Washington, D.C. Hereafter referred to as alien enemy problem memo.

2. Missoula (Mont.) *Missoulian*, 1 April 1941.

3. *Missoulian*, 7 May 1941.

4. "U.S. Uses First Force To Win Bloodless Victory In Battle Of The Atlantic," *Life*, 14 April 1941, p. 23.

5. Ibid.

6. Alien enemy problem memorandum, p. 3.

7. Ibid.

8. Patsy Sumie Saiki, *Ganbare! An Example of Japanese Spirit* (Honolulu: Kisaku, Inc., 1982), p. 128.

9. Untitled memorandum in regard to Western Hemisphere Conference, 24 July 1943, National Archives. Hereafter referred to as Western Hemisphere memorandum.

10. Letter to W.F. Kelly, chief of the Immigration and Naturalization Service, from N.D. Collaer, supervisor of alien detentions, 4 May 1941, as cited by Susan Buchel, in unpublished manuscript "Bella Vista," p. 3, 1980, University of Montana Archives, Missoula, Mont.

11. Letter from Robert P. Patterson to Attorney General Robert H. Jackson, 15 July 1941, as cited by Buchel, p. 7.

12. Buchel, p. 6.

13. Western Hemisphere memorandum, p. 5.

14. Umberto Benedetti, interview by author, 1 April 1987, Missoula, Montana. Benedetti stayed in Missoula after the war and was for many years employed at the University of Montana Print Shop.

15. *Missoula Sentinel*, 8 May 1941. The Sentinel was the afternoon edition of the *Missoulian*.

16. *Missoulian*, 10 May 1941.

17. Ibid.

18. *Missoula Sentinel*, 9 May 1941.

19. *Missoulian*, 10 May 1941.

20. *Missoulian*, 11 May 1941.

21. *Missoulian*, 11 May 1941.

22. *Missoulian*, 17 May 1941.

23. Alien enemy problem memorandum, p. 5.

24. *Missoulian*, 15 June 1941.

25. Benedetti interview.

26. *Missoulian*, 15 June 1941.

27. Letter to N.D. Collaer from Jerry Mangione, 20 June 1944, National Archives. This report was not made at the time of the incident. Rather, it is included in anecdotal material at the Archives that was requested by Immigration Service headquarters as it began to close the camps near the end of the war.

CHAPTER TWO

1. Alfredo Cipolato interview by Bill Lang, 9 January 1981, Missoula, tape recording. Montana Historical Society, Helena. Cipolato now owns the Broadway Market in Missoula.

2. Jerre Mangione, *An Ethnic at Large: A Memoir of America in the Thirties and Forties* (New York: G.P. Putnam and Sons, 1978), p. 343.

3. Ibid., pp. 343–344.

4. Letter from Nick Collaer to Immigration Service, April 13, 1942, as cited by Susan Buchel, unpublished manuscript "Bella Vista," p. 23, 1980, University of Montana Archives, Missoula, Montana.

5. Ibid., pp. 23–24.

6. Mangione, p. 344.

7. *New York Times*, 6 August 1941.

8. Ibid.

9. *Corriere D'America—Domenica*, New York, 17 August 1941.

10. *Il Progresso*, as quoted in the *New York Times*, 13 August 1941.

11. "News From Montana," *Time*, 18 August 1941, p. 24.

12. *Missoulian*, 6 July 1941.

13. *Missoulian*, 7 August 1941.

14. Department of Justice memorandum, "Internment Camps Operated by the U.S. Immigration and Naturalization Service," 24 July 1943, Record Group 85, Box 4, File 3, National Archives.

15. Letter from Frank Brown to Bert Fraser, 19 November 1942, as cited by Buchel, p. 16.

16. Buchel, p. 11.

17. *Missoulian*, 1 October 1941.

18. Mangione, p. 345.

19. Cipolato interview.

20. Lyle Slade interview by Julie Kenfield, 1979, Missoula, tape recording. University of Montana Archives, Missoula, Montana.

21. Cipolato interview.

22. *Missoulian*, 22 July 1941.

23. *Missoulian*, 15 August 1941.

24. *Missoulian*, 7 August 1941.

25. *Missoulian*, 1 October 1941.

26. Umberto Benedetti, *The Lifestyle of Italian Internees at Fort Missoula, Montana, 1941–1943* (Missoula, Montana: University of Montana), p. 36.

27. Ibid., p. 44, and interview with Benedetti, 2 March 1995.

28. *Missoulian*, 1 October 1941.

29. *Missoulian*, 7 August 1941.

30. Slade interview.

31. Internment Camp Operation memo, p. 5.

32. Mangione, p. 344.

33. Ibid.

34. Letter to the United States Surgeon General from Frank Brown, as cited by Buchel, p. 17.

35. *Missoulian*, 12 December 1941.

CHAPTER THREE

1. Commission on Wartime Relocation and Internment of Civilians, "Personal Justice Denied" (Washington, D.C.: Government Printing Office, 1982), p. 31.

2. Ibid., p. 38.

3. Ibid.

4. Ibid., p. 29

5. Ibid., p. 32.

6. Dan K. Inouye with Lawrence Elliot, *Journey to Washington* (Englewood Cliff, N.J.: Prentice-Hall, 1967), pp. 36–37.

7. Roger Daniels, *The Politics of Prejudice* (Berkeley, University of California Press, 1962), p. 10.

8. Peter Irons, *Justice at War* (New York: Oxford University Press, 1983), p. 10.

9. Masakazu Iwata, *Planted in Good Soil*, p. 258, as cited by Daniels, p. 10.

10. Irons, p. 20.

11. Ibid., p. 22.

12. John Tateishi, *And Justice for All* (New York: Random House, 1984) p. 52.

13. "Report on an article by Commissioner Harrison in the May [1942] issue of Survey Graphic," unsigned, undated, Record Group 85, Box 3, File 3, National Archives, Washington, D.C.

14. Report by Curtis B. Munson, "Japanese on the West Coast," November 7, 1941, as quoted by the Commission on Wartime Relocation and Internment of Civilians, *Personal Justice Denied*, p. 53.

15. Survey Graphic report.

16. Tateishi, p. 33.

17. Ibid., pp. 34–35.

18. Ibid., p. 34.

19. Ibid., pp. 16–17.

20. Ibid., p. 62–63.

21. Irons, p. 81.

22. Tateishi, p. 85.

23. Ibid., p. 64.

CHAPTER FOUR

1. *Missoulian*, 28 March 1942.

2. *Missoulian*, 9 December 1941.

3. Dave Walter, "From fear to trust in World War II," *Montana Magazine*, January-February 1987, pp. 63–70.

4. *Missoulian*, 14 December 1941.

5. *Missoulian*, 16 December 1941.

6. *Personal Justice Denied*, p. 55.

7. Ibid.

8. *Missoulian*, 19 December 1941.

9. *Missoulian*, 30 December 1941.

10. Clyde Neu interview by Julie Kenfield, 19 February 1984, University of Montana Archives, Missoula.

11. *Missoulian*, 19 December 1941.

12. *Missoulian*, 20 December 1941.

13. Statistics from Fort Missoula file, Record Group 85, Boxes 1–5, National Archives.

14. *Christian Advocate*, 26 March 1942.

15. Sigrid Aren, "Italian, Japanese Internees Won't Eat Together," Wide World, 8 August 1942.

16. Jere Mangione, *An Ethnic at Large* (New York: G. P. Putnam's Sons, 1978), p. 347.

17. Patsy Sumie Saiki, *Ganbare! An Example of Japanese Spirit* (Honolulu: Kisaku, Inc., 1982) p. 129.

18. Ibid.

19. Ibid., p. 131.

20. *Missoulian*, 9 February 1942.

21. Ibid.

22. *Missoulian*, 9 February 1942.

23. *Missoulian*, 4 March 1942.

24. Michi Weglyn, *Years of Infamy: The Untold Story of America's Concentration Camps* (New York: William Morrow and Sons, 1976), p. 37.

25. *Missoulian*, 18 February 1942.

26. *Missoulian*, 27 February 1942.

27. *Missoulian*, 25 February 1942.

28. *Missoulian*, 3 March 1942.

29. *Missoulian*, 7 March 1942.

30. *Missoulian*, 1 April 1942.

31. *Missoulian*, 8 June 1942.

CHAPTER FIVE

1. Report of the Commission on Wartime Relocation and Internment of Civilians, "Personal Justice Denied" (Washington, D.C.: GPO, 1983), pp. 98–99.

2. Frank F. Chuman, *The Bamboo People: The Law and Japanese-Americans* (Del Mar, California: Publisher's Inc., 1976), p. 151.

3. Ibid., p. 150.

4. Hearings, 77th Congress, 2nd sess. Select Committee Investigating National Defense Migration (Washington: Government Printing Office, 1942), as quoted by Michi Weglyn, *Years of Infamy: The Untold Story of America's Concentration Camps* (New York: William Morrow and Sons, 1976), p. 38.

5. *Washington Post*, 15 February 1942, as quoted by Peter Irons, *Justice at War*.

6. A Freedom of Information request for copies of those transcripts was made by the author of this book in 1983 but the Justice Department

replied in 1984 that it could not find any such transcripts in its files. Letter to author from Mark T. Sheehan, assistant director, Office of Public Affairs, Department of Justice, Washington, D.C., 6 March 1984.

7. *Missoulian*, 15 February 1942.

8. John Tateishi, *And Justice For All* (New York: Random House, 1984), p. 67.

9. Ibid., pp. 67–68.

10. Betty E. Mitson, "Friend Herbert: Concern in Action Within America's Concentration Camps" (Master's thesis, California State University, Fullerton, 1975) p. 10.

11. Ibid., p.12.

12. Ibid., p. 12–13.

13. Ibid., p. 13.

14. Ibid., pp. 14–15.

15. *Missoulian*, 15 February 1942.

16. Ibid.

17. Ibid.

18. *Missoula Sentinel*, 25 February 1942.

19. *Missoulian*, 29 June 1942.

20. *Great Falls Tribune*, 13 August 1942.

21. *Missoulian*, 24 March 1942.

22. *Missoulian*, 6 April 1942.

23. *Missoulian*, 12 April 1942.

24. Howard Toole to Governor Sam C. Ford, 13 April 1942, Gov. Sam C. Ford Administration Papers, Manuscript Collection 35, Box 107, Folder 4, Montana Historical Society Archives, Helena, Mont.

25. Montana American Legion Resolution, undated, Ford Papers, Box 107, Folder 4, Montana Historical Society Archives, Helena, Mont.

26. Anaconda Commercial Club Resolution, 12 April 1942, Ford Papers, Box 107, Folder 104, Montana Historical Society, Helena, Mont.

27. *Missoula Sentinel*, 14 April 1942.

28. *Missoulian*, 14 July 1942.

29. *Missoulian*, 23 July 1942.

30. *Missoulian*, 26 July 1942.

31. *Missoulian*, 29 July 1942.

32. *Missoulian*, 24 March 1942.

CHAPTER SIX

1. Testimony of Herman F. Schwandt, acting inspector in charge of Detention and Deportation Division, Seattle, before District Director R.P. Bonham, Seattle, 2 June 1942, Record Group 85, Box 1, File Part I, National Archives, Washington, D.C.

2. Report to Attorney General and Solicitor General from Immigration and Naturalization Commissioner Earl G. Harrison, 29 August 1942, Record Group 85, Box 2, File March 1943, National Archives, Washington, D.C.

3. Transcripts of Reports of Investigation Under Immigration Laws, Umeo Miyagishima, Yonezo Miyagishima, Ito Yenkichi, Ikuichi Imada, Nobu Watanabe, Fred Shizutaro Toyota, Gizo Oikawa, and Toraki Tinomita, Record Group No. 85, Box 2, March 1943, National Archives, Washington, D.C.

4. Report of investigation by Ernest J. Hover to Joseph Savoretti, June 11, 1942, Record Group 85, Box 1, File Part I, National Archives, Washington, D.C. Hereafter referred to as Hover report.

5. Report of Investigation Under Immigration Laws, Gizo Oikawa, Fort Missoula, Montana, March 9, 1942, Record Group 85, Box 2, File March 1943, National Archives, Washington, D.C.

6. Report of Investigation Under Immigration Laws, Yanezo Miyagishima, File No. 1036/1873, February 20 and 24, 1942, Fort Missoula, Montana, Record Group 85, Box 2, File March 1943, National Archives, Washington, D.C.

7. Letter to W. Kelly from Walter S. Bliss, June 9, 1942, Record Group 85, Box 2, File March 1943, National Archives, Washington, D.C.

8. Memorandum of Walter S. Bliss, June 4, 1942. Prepared in defense of charges of mistreatment. Record Group 85, Box 2, File March 1943, National Archives, Washington, D.C.

9. Transcript of interview with Harold W. Brown by Judson F. Shaw, acting district director, Los Angeles district, Immigration and Naturalization Service, at Fort Missoula, Montana, June 5, 1942, p. 7. Record Group 85, Box 1, Part I, National Archives, Washington, D.C.

10. Report of Investigation Under Immigration Laws, Ito Yenkichi, Fort Missoula, Montana, March 10, 1942, Record Group 85, Box 2, File March 1943, National Archives, Washington, D.C.

11. Ibid.

12. Bliss memo of June 4, 1942.

13. Ibid.

14. Ibid.

15. Walter Bliss testimony before examining officer Karl I. Zimmerman, 18 June 1942, p. 10. Record Group 85, Box 1, File Part I, National Archives, Washington, D.C.

16. Ibid., p. 6.

17. Ibid.

18. Ibid., p. 17.

19. Clyde Neu interview by Julie Kenfield, 19 February 1984, tape recording, University of Montana Archives, Missoula, Mont.

20. Statement of Clyde Neu in investigation into mistreatment of Japanese at Fort Missoula, Montana, 6 June 1942, Record Group 85, Box 1, File Part III, National Archives, Washington, D.C.

21. Testimony of Clarence V. Carlson before Karl I. Zimmerman, 14 June 1942, Fort Missoula, Montana, Record Group 85, Box 1, File No. Part III, National Archives, Washington, D.C.

22. Testimony of Leonard Kuka before W. Kelly, 6 June 1942, Fort Missoula, Montana, Record Group 85, Box 1, File No. Part III, National Archives, Washington, D.C.

23. Testimony of John Harrington to W. Kelly, 6 June 1942, Fort Missoula, Montana, Record Group 85, Box 1, File Part I, National Archives, Washington, D.C.

24. Testimony of Thomas Bayles before W. Kelly, 6 June 1942, Fort Missoula, Montana, Record Group 85, Box 1, File Part 1, National Archives, Washington, D.C.

25. Ibid.

26. Report concerning allegations of mistreatment of Japanese aliens at Fort Missoula, Montana, and Fort Lincoln, North Dakota, by Karl Zimmerman, 29 June 1942, Record Group 85, Box 2, File March 1943, National Archives, Washington, D.C.

27. Memorandum for the Attorney General and the Solicitor General from Commissioner Earl G. Harrison, 29 August 1942, Record Group 85, Box 2, File March 1943, National Archives, Washington, D.C.

28. Letter from Burton K. Wheeler to Attorney General Francis Biddle, 26 June 1942, citing statements from Campbell, Record Group 85, Box 2, File March 1943, National Archives, Washington, D.C.

CHAPTER SEVEN

1. Statistics from Fort Missoula, Montana, detention camp files, Record Group 85, Boxes 1 and 2, National Archives, Washington, D.C.

2. Letter from Yahei Taoka to Nick Collaer, 16 May 1942, Record Group 85, Box 2, File March 1943, National Archives, Washington, D.C.

3. Jere Mangione, *An Ethnic at Large* (New York: G. P. Putnam's Sons, 1978, pp. 346–47.

4. Interview of Arthur Deschamps by Susan Buchel, November 20, 1979, University of Montana Archives, Missoula, Montana.

5. Ibid.

6. Ibid.

7. *Helena Independent*, March 2, 1942, p. 3.

8. *Missoulian*, April 11, 1942.

9. *Malta (Montana) Phillips County News*, February 26, 1942, as cited by Dave Walter in "From fear to trust in World War II," *Montana Magazine*, January-February 1987, p. 67.

10. *Great Falls Tribune*, April 30, 1942.

11. Ibid.

12. Wire, Northern Montana Beet Growers Association to Senator B. K. Wheeler, May 6, 1942, OF 197-A, Franklin D. Roosevelt Library, as quoted by Michi Weglyn in Years of Infamy: The Untold Story of America's Concentration Camps, (New York: William Morrow and Company, Inc., 1976), p. 98.

13. Letter, Senator James Murray to M.H. McIntyre, September 24, 1942, OF 197-A, FDR Library, as quoted by Weglyn.

14. Unsigned memorandum, "Partial List of Sites for Detention Camps or Stations Inspected by Officers or Offered for Use as Camps," October 1, 1942, Record Group 85, Box 1, File March 1943, National Archives, Washington, D.C.

15. Deschamps interview by Buchel.

16. Donald Wright, "The Japanese-American in Montana in World War II," senior paper in journalism, University of Montana School of Journalism, 1968, p. 18.

17. *Missoulian*, April 11, 1942.

18. *Missoulian*, May 23, 1942.

19. *Missoulian*, June 5, 1942.

20. *Missoulian*, June 30, 1942.

21. *Missoulian*, August 26, 1942.

22. *Missoulian*, October 10, 1942.

23. *Missoulian*, December 5, 1942.

24. *Missoulian*, July 1, 1943.

25. *Missoulian*, July 9, 1943.

26. *Missoulian*, July 9, 1943.

27. *Missoulian*, July 28, 1943.

28. Ibid.

29. *Missoulian*, July 29, 1943.

30. *Missoulian*, September 9, 1943.

31. Memorandum to United States Attorney General Francis Biddle from Ugo Carusi, Immigration Service commissioner, August 24, 1945, Record Group 85, Box 5, File 2, National Archives, Washington, D.C.

Afterword

1. Patsy Sumie Saiki, *Ganbare! An Example of Japanese Spirit* (Honolulu: Kisaku, Inc., 1982), p. 133.

2. *Missoulian*, Oct. 26, 1994, p. B1.

Model ship made by an Italian detainee, 1942. MONTANA HISTORICAL SOCIETY

APPENDIX

FOLLOWING ARE PHOTOCOPIES of government documents from Department of Justice files that were opened to the public for the first time in 1985.

The significance of the nearly 400 names on these lists can only be left to speculation. However, government files show that some men interned at Fort Missoula were permitted to join their families at internment camps opened and operated by the newly created War Relocation Authority beginning in the spring of 1942. The names of the Fort Missoula Japanese represent those who were not allowed to rejoin their families, but who were transferred to other camps operated by the Immigration and Naturalization Service. Because these men remained in the custody of the Justice Department, one might conclude that they were the men who, after loyalty hearings at Fort Missoula, were determined possible threats and kept separate from the American Japanese community.

JAPANESE INTERNED AT FORT SILL, OKLAHOMA, FROM FORT MISSOULA, MONTANA

ABE, Arakichi

AIHARA, Seikichi

AKAYAMA, Tomokichi

AKITA, Uhiji

AKUTAGAWA, Kiyoshi

AOKI, Kamenosuke

AOYAMA, Minoru

ASANO, Kintaro

ASAKURA, Junji

ASAKAWA, Hachisaku

AZUMA, Yu

AZUMANO, Hatsutaro

BAN, Takeshi (Dr)

BESSHO, Gentaro

BUNJA, Shiro

CHIBA, Magojiro

CHINO, Tsuneji

DAIGO, Keitaro

DATE, Naminosuke

EDO, Kinjiro

ETO, Tameji

FUJII, Touroku

FUJITA, Masakatsu

FUKUDA, Kentaro

FUKUDA, Yozo

FURUKAWA, Enta

FURUSAWA, Takashi

FURUTA, Shiroichi

GOTO, Isao

HAMA, Yosaburo

HAMAGUCHI, Heizaburo

HANAKI, Eizo

HANDA, Itaro

HARADA, Takashi

HASHIMOTO, Kazuichi

HASUIKE, George Susumu

HATA, Goro

HATAKEYAMA, Kikuji

HATANAKA, Yoshisuke

HATASHITA, Teizo

HIGASHI, Kiyusaburo

HIGASHI, Toyokichi

HIMAKA, Chosuke

HIRABAYASHI, Hamao

HIRAGA, Jusho

JAPS - FORT SILL

HIRAO, Kengo (Kane)	ISHII, Chuhei
HIRAO, Tomiji	ISHII, Tsurataro
HIRAOKA, Matsumi	ISHIZAWA, Chiyohachi
HIRATA, Frank Kazuma	ITAHARA, Kumashige
HIRAYAMA, Bunjiro	ITAMI, Asegoro
HORAGAMI, Nichizo	ITO, Hichijiro
HORI, Isaburo	ITO, Michio
HORI, Kishiro	ITO, Naotaro
HOSHIKO, Hitoshi	IWANAGA, Tomoki
	IWATA, Kametaro
IBA, Shoichi	IWATA, Ryoichi
IIZUKA, Shotaro	
IKEDA, Bunen	KAGAWA, Shotaro
IKEDA, Kawando	KAI, Masajiro
IKEDA, Naoichi	KAJIKAWA, Iwanari
IKEYA, Kaiji	KAJIWARA, Rinzaburo
IMADA, Ikuichi	KAME, Kameniro
IMAHASHI, Shigeji	KAMIBAYASHI, Hanbei
IMAI, Seizo	KAMIYA, Matsutaro
INOUYE, Hikohashi	KANAGAE, Katsuzo
INOUYE, Hokichi	KANEKO, Junji
INOUYE, Kikuji	KANEKO, Kurakichi
INUZUKA, Takashi	KARIYA, Hiroshi
ISEDA, Gyosuke	KASAI, Henry Yoshihiko
ISHIBASHI, Naoichi	KASAI, Umenosuke
ISHIDA, Bishop Nitten	KATAOKA, Ichiro
ISHIDA, Tazo Tom	KATO, Meitoku

-2-

JAPS - FORT SILL

KATO, Tokichi

KATO, Tomosaburo

KATO, Toyataro

KATO, Yahichi

KAWADA, Shigenaga

KAWAGUCHI, Asakichi

KAWAGUCHI, Shojiro

KAWAHARA, Koichi

KIMURA, Dotatsu

KINOSHITA, Sadashichi

KISHIMA, Shunichi

KISO, Iichi

KITA, Taiji

KIYAMA, Soshiro

KIZU, Yoshimatsu

KOBAYASHI, Makio

KOBAYASHI, Takio

KOBAYASHI, Toraichi

KOHARA, Sadeji

KOISO, Tetsunosuke

KOMAI, H. Toyosaku

KONDO, Saburo Hirashima

KONO, Isamu

KONO, Katsuya

KONO, Toraichi

KOYAMA, Keizaburo

KOYAMA, Shiroichi

KOZIMA, Gitaro

KUBOTA, Fukumatsu

KUBOTA, Sakutaro

KUGA, Jihei

KUMAMOTO, Shusuke

KURATOMI, Rintaro

KUSANO, Yasutaro

KUSUMOTO, Joy R.

KUWATA, George Minori

MAEHARA, Kameichi

MARUOKA, Shigematsu

MARUYAMA, Eizo

MARUYAMA, Tohachiro

MASHIKO, Shinobu

MASUOKA, Baiichi

MATSUSHITA, Yukichi

MATSUDAIRA, Ichiro

MATSUDO, Yorisuke

MATSUMOTO, Hajime

MATSUURA, Masaji

MAYEKAWA, George Teijiro

MICHIDA, Yaichi

MINAMI, Nobuichi

MINAMI, Yaemon

MINAMINO, Rikichi

JAPS - FORT SILL

MITANI, Masayoshi

MIURA, Koshiro

MIWA, Nakazo

MIYAKE, Tanzo

MIYAKO, Kozo

MIWAGAWA, Frank Jukichi

MIYATA, Kumao

MIZUKAMI, Bunkishi Harry

MIZUKI, Kashitaro

MOMII, Kizemon Ikken

MORIGUCHI, Nobuyuki

MORINAGA, Kaoru

MUKAEDA, Katsuma

MURAKAMI, Jinkichi

MURANAKA, Eiichi

MURAOKA, Saburo

MURATA, Shunichi

MUTOW, Kichitaro

NAGAISHI, Gengo

NAGAMATSU, Ikugoro

NAGAMINE, Haruyuki

NAGANO, Kiro

NAGASAKI, Toyokichi

NAGASE, Yoshio Masaomi

NAKADATE, Yojiro

NAKAGAWA, Kosaburo

NAKAGAWA, Shintaro

NAKAHARA, James Toshiharau

NAKAHATA, Shiro Y.

NAKAMICHI, Kosaku

NAKAMURA, Akimatsu

NAKAMURA, Gongoro

NAKAMURA, Kyutaro

NAKAMURA, Naoshi

NAKAMURA, Tatsuji

NAKAMURA, Yoshio

NAKANO, Kiyoshi

NAKATSUKA, Kinsaburo

NARUMI, Jutaro

NASE, Masao

NIMURA, Yoshitsugo

NISHI, Kinji

NISHI, Mojuro

NISHIMOTO, Teijiro

NISHIMURA, Sueji

NISHINA, Seizo

NISHINO, Mitsunari

NISHIYAMA, Matsujuro

NISHIZO, Shinjiro

NONOGUCHI, Chiyoichi

NORITAKE, Hatsuo (Motoo)

-4-

JAPS - FORT SILL

OBAYSHI, Joe Uichiro

OGATA, Sueo

OGURA, Ukichi

OHARA, Shozo

OHEI, Kinzo

OISHI, Yojiro

OKAMOTO, Hisajiro

OKAMURA, Suyeichi

OKAZAKI, Shigeo

OKUNO, Bunshichi

OKURA, Momota

OKUYAMA, Eitaro

ONISHI, Junichi

ONO, Kameichi Frank

OSAKI, Junji

OTOI, Masunosuke

OTAKE, Tamaichi

OYE, Kumejiro

OZAKI, Kamesaburo

RIKIMARU, Isamu

RIKIMARU, Mataji

SAKABU, Kansaku

SAKAINO, Bunro

SAKAKURA, Kotaro

SAKAUE, Sokuma

SAKIMURA, Masaichi

SAKOGAWA, Itsuji

SAKURADA, Jisaku

SASAHARA, Yoshita Yoshitaro

SASAKI, Kosaku

SASAKI, Shozo

SASAKI, Shunji

SASAME, Takashi

SATA, Hijime

SATO, Ichio

SATO, Meitoku

SATO, Mikitaro

SATO, Rikitaro

SATO, Takeo

SATO, Zentaro

SEKI, Kyoichiro

SEKIYAMA, Isami

SHIBATA, Shin

SHIMA, Hynosuke

SHIMADA, Kanetaro

SHIMASAKI, Taichiro

SHIMIZU, Mitsuhiko

SHIMODA, Itsuji

SHINOZAKI, Kenjiro

SHINTANI, Ritsusuke

SHIOKAWA, Tomio

SHIOTA, Takezo

JAPS - FORT SILL

SHIRAKAWA, Choichiro

SHIRAKAWA, Tokio

SHIODE, Shoichi

SUGANO, Tomikichi

SUGIMURA, Mankichi

SUGINO, Masami

SUMI, Toraichi

SUMINAGA, Konosuke

SUTO, Sataro

SUYAMA, Yasugoro

SUZUKI, Asakichi

SUZUKI, Bunichi

SUZUKI, Hiroshi

TABATA, Sam Sokichi

TACHIBANA, Chikamori

TADA, Kinichi

TAGUMA, Asatoshi

TAKAHASHI, Giichi

TAKAHASHI, Shodo Seytsu

TAKAHASHI, Terusone

TAKAHASHI, Wataru

TAKAKI, Umekichi

TAKAO, Fusakichi

TAKAO, Inosuke

TAKASE, Yutaka

TAKATA, Giichi

TAKEICHI, Masato
TAKEMOTO, Yasuo

TAKEMURA, Seiji

TAKEOKA, Daiichi

TAMARI, Shinnosuke

TAMBARA, Asakichi

TANAKA, Kakuo

TANAKA, Masayashi

TANAKA, Sadamatsu

TANAKA, Yasutaro

TANIGUCHI, Miake

TAOKA, Yahei

TATEISHI, Yoshimasa

TATEOKA, Harry Hisashi

TATSUNO, Ryuji

TERAO, Ichiro

TOGURI, Makoto

TOKUYAMA, Jitsutaro (Mitaro)

TOMA, Tsurumatsu

TOMIHIRO, Senichi

TOMIO, Harry Tomozo

TOMOOKA, Toyokichi

TONAI, Genoro

TOSHIMA, Isao

TOYAMA, Takeo

TOYOTA, Fred S.

TSUBOI, Teruo

TSUDA, Mokuryu

-6-

JAPS - FORT SILL

TSUDA, Noboru

TSUJI, Iwao

TSUMAGARI, Takeji

UCHIYAMA, Keijiro

UDO, Tsunejiro

UEHARA, Tokuya

URUSHIBATA, Kojiro

USUDA, Masaoki

UYEJI, Kintaro

UYEMURA, Katsuji

UYENO, Hampei

UYENO, Tomoichi

UYESUGI, Seikichi

WADA, Konosuke

WAKAYAMA, Katsuichi Tom

WATANABE, Masataro

WATANABE, Nobu

WATANABE, Tomoichi

WATANABE, Yozo

WATANUKI, Mitsugoro

YABE, Giiti

YAMADA, Jutaro

YAMAHIRO, Nisuke

YAMAMATO, Gengo

YAMAMOTO, Masamichi D.

YAMAMOTO, Hisataro

YAMAMOTO, Yotaro

YAMANOUCHI, Teijiro

YAMASHITA, Gihachi

YAMASHITA, Toshimi

YAMATAMI, Kosaku

YAMAWAKI, Genkichi

YASUI, Masuo

YASUI, Ryoichi Johnny

YOSHII, Eisaku

YOSHIKAWA, Toyokichi

YOSHIMURA, Kichigoro

YOSHINAKA, Seiichi

YOSHITOMI, Junichi Joe

YUASA, Fukukichi

JAPS INTERNED AT FORT SAM HOUSTON, TEXAS, FROM FORT MISSOULA, MONTANA

ABE, Shungo

AMANO, James Masatoku

ANDO, Sadajiro

AOKI, Shigeru

DATE, Noboru

DOIGUCHI, Suketaro

FUJII, Hanjiro

FUKADA, Chosaburo

FUKADA, Yoshiaki

HOSHINO, Reiji

HYODO, Masakazu Frank

KATO, Toyanaga

KUWATA, Syoiti

MAKINO, Tamotsa

MIDZUNO, Hiroishi

MITSUNAGA, Junsaku Joe

MIYAHARA, Eizoh

NAKAO, Sachio

NAKANO, Sakutaro

NAKAMURA, Otonosuke

NISHII, Guzei

NISHIMURA, Ikuzo

NOZAKA, Shigeharu

OISHI, Ishimatsu

SAKAI, Masaji James

SAKATA, Kameki

SHIMADA, Senkibhi

SHIMIZU, Iwajiro Frank

SHINODA, Ryoichi

SUGIYAMA, Katsujiro

TADATOSHI, Tsuji

TAKIGUCHI, Keijiro

TETSUZO, Sawataki

UNO, Sohichi

URANO, Hajimu

WAKASA, Kazuo

YAMAGUCHI, Tadashi

YAMAMOTO, Eiichi (Roy)

YASUMURA, Teikichi

YOSHIZAWA, Seizo

German nationals at Fort Missoula, Montana.
This list is from the National Archives.

R.W. Becker
Walter Eurich
Armand Gregoire
Hans Hartmann
Gerhardt Kaempfer
Alfred Kerstens
Robert Krefft
Herbert Mallnow
F.W. Menke
Heinrich Mohrdieck
Ernst Muehlbrett
August Ossendorf
Walter Potrzeba
William Potting
Horst von Rhoden
Nick Scoflick
Wilhelm Stein
Hans Stiewe
Herbert Suessbach
Otto Tornach
Erwin Wendlandt
Paul Wischenewski

Two Immigration and Naturalization Service officers talk with an Italian who was on work parole at a western Montana farm. MONTANA HISTORICAL SOCIETY

**1942 view of the
Detention Camp. It was
during the first six
months of this year that
the detainee population
was at its highest.**
HISTORICAL MUSEUM AT
FORT MISSOULA

BIBLIOGRAPHY

BOOKS

Benedetti, Umberto. *The Lifestyle of Italian Internees at Fort Missoula, Montana, 1941–1943.* Missoula, Mont.: University of Montana, 1986.

Chuman, Frank F. *The Bamboo People: The Law and Japanese Americans.* Del Mar, Calif.: Publisher's Inc., 1976.

Cohen, Stan. *V for Victory, America's Home Front During World War II.* Missoula, Mont.: Pictorial Histories Publishing Co., 1991.

Commission on Wartime Relocation and Internship of Civilians. *Personal Justice Denied.* Washington, D.C.: United States Government Printing Office, 1982.

Daniels, Roger. *Concentration Camps USA: Japanese Americans and World War II.* New York: Holt, Rinehart and Winston, Inc., 1972.

———. *The Politics of Prejudice.* Berkeley: University of California Press, 1962.

Grodzins, Morton. *Americans Betrayed: Politics and the Japanese Evacuation.* Chicago: University of Chicago Press, 1949.

Hosokawa, Bill. *Nisei: The Quiet Americans.* New York: William Morrow & Co., 1969.

Inouye, Dan K., with Lawrence Elliot. *Journey to Washington.* Englewood Cliffs, N.J.: Prentice-Hall, 1967.

Irons, Jeremy. *Justice at War.* New York: Oxford University Press, 1982.

McWilliams, Carey. *Prejudice.* Boston: Little, Brown and Co., 1985.

Saiki, Patsy Sumi. *Ganbare! An Example of Japanese Spirit.* Honolulu: Kisaku, Inc., 1982.

Tateishi, John. *And Justice For All.* New York: Random House, 1984.

tenBroek, Jacobus, Edward N. Barnhart and Floyd Matson. *Prejudice, War and the Constitution.* Berkeley: University of California Press, 1954.

Terkel, Studs. *The Good War: An Oral History of World War Two.*

Weglyn, Michi. *Years of Infamy: The Untold Story of America's Concentration Camps.* New York: William Morrow and Sons, 1976.

NEWSPAPERS

Great Falls Tribune, 1941–43.
Missoulian, 1941–44, 1983–88.
Missoula Sentinel, 1941–44.
New York Times, 1941–42.

ARTICLES

Oishi, Gene. "The Anxiety of Being A Japanese-American." *New York Times Magazine.*, 28 April 1985.

"News From Montana." *Time*, 18 August 1941.

"U.S. Uses First Force To Win Bloodless Victory In Battle Of The Atlantic." *Life*, 14 April 1941.

Walter, Dave. "From fear to trust in World War II." *Montana Magazine*, January–February 1987, 63–70.

UNPUBLISHED MANUSCRIPTS

Buchel, Susan. "Bella Vista." Unpublished manuscript. University of Montana Archives. Missoula, 1980.

Johnson, Stuart. "The Treatment of German-Americans in World War I and Japanese Americans in World War II." Senior paper in journalism, University of Montana, 1978.

Mitson, Betty. "Friend Herbert: Concern in Action Within America's Concentration Camps." Master's thesis, California State University, Fullerton, 1975.

Wright, Donald. "The Japanese-American in Montana World War II." Senior paper in journalism, University of Montana, 1968.

INTERVIEWS

Bell, Mary. Interview by Julie Kenfield, December 1979. Oral History Collection, University of Montana Archives, Missoula, Montana.

Benedetti, Umberto. Missoula, Montana. 1 April 1987.

Cipolato, Alfredo. Interview by Bill Lang, 9 January 1981. Oral History Collection, Montana Historical Society, Helena.

Deschamps, Arthur. Interview by Susan Buchel, 20 November 1979. Oral History Collection, University of Montana Archives, Missoula, Montana.

Neu, Clyde. Interview by Julie Kenfield, 19 February 1984. Oral History Collection, University of Montana Archives, Missoula, Montana.

Slade, Lyle. Interview by Julie Kenfield, 3 December 1979. Oral History Collection, University of Montana Archives, Missoula, Montana.

Manuscript Collections

Montana Historical Society Archives. Governor Sam C. Ford Administration Papers, Manuscript Collection 35, Box 107.

United States Government Documents

United States Department of Justice. Fort Missoula Alien Detention Camp Files. Record Group 85, Boxes 1–4. National Archives, Washington, D.C.

ABOUT THE AUTHOR

CAROL BULGER VAN VALKENBURG is a native Montanan and an associate professor of journalism at the University of Montana in Missoula. She worked for 10 years as a reporter, editor and editorial writer at *The Missoulian* and spends occasional summers on the copy desk at *The Philadelphia Inquirer*. When she's not teaching or writing she spends her days fishing.